Walking Home

Carol Marchal Storrer
with Vicki Hesterman

AUGSBURG Publishing House • Minneapolis

WALKING HOME

Scripture quotations unless otherwise noted are from the King James
Version.

Photos: Vicki Hesterman, cover, p. 144B, 145A, 145B, 145C

With much love to

Mom and Dad
Bob and Charlene Lantz
Jeffrey

And most of all, to Tom

Special thanks to

Vicki Hesterman, who encouraged me to gather my thoughts, experiences, and medical data for this book. She made sense of it all.

David Rupp Jr. for carefully checking the manuscript and for all his time and assistance.

My sisters and brothers, Margie Busch, Judy Cron, Darlene McClurg, Diane Cyrier, Pat Clevenger, Theresa, Mike and Francis Marchal.

Tom's parents and sisters, Ed and Ruth Storrer, Nancy Sindlinger, Diane Kruse, Linda Martin, Susie Spielman, Mary Schnitkey, and Dave and Dan Storrer.

ACKNOWLEDGMENTS

For their continuous encouragement and help as this book was being organized and written, a special thank-you from co-author Vicki Hesterman to Vern and Phyllis Hesterman, Linda and Randy Ridley, Sue and Steve Hurst, Bob and Tom Hesterman, Lynn Myking Mitchell, and Nicole Danison. Thanks also to Dr. V. Michael Holers for checking the manuscript for medical accuracy, and to Pastors Vance Knutsen, Gene Holtz and Bill Sy for helping with theological questions. Special thanks to the staff at Augsburg Publishing House for their enthusiasm and help.

For their love, concern, and prayers, from Carol Storrer, a big thank-you to all those who cared about me and my family during our trying times. I want you all to know that I appreciate every prayer and every act of kindness. I saw Christian love in action, and it made a tremendous difference in my life.

Those mentioned in the book whom I also want to thank include Dr. Dale Mull and Dr. Joe Targonski for their extra help, Mary Ellen Stuckey, Theo Yoder, Evelyn Schmucker, Katharina Myers, Cynthia Varner, Linda Garmon, Russ and Janis Watson, Bud and Gert Hitt and Gil and Rose Lewis. Thanks to nursing volunteers Joan Aschliman, Wilma Beck, Donna Buehrer, Jane Fielitz, Deb Grieser, Barb Graf, Carol Hackett, Sylvia Holland, Diane Thrasher Kruse, Lynne Leu, Bev Nelson, and Deb Short. For their encouragement and practical help, thanks to Mrs. Lyle Friesen, Betty Grieser, Rita Kruse, Dorothy Nafziger, Pearl Stuckey, Marlene Graf, Marlene Beck, Father Clement Alt,

Doris Beck, Ann Ernst, Joy Link, Dave and Sharon Rex, Helen Weldy, Richard and Mary Etta Lauber, Tim Dominique, Pauline Lantz, Patti Nichols, Marlene Coressel, Jewel Taylor, Eldora Marshall, Dawn Wyse, Myrt Leininger, Dale and Eleanor Rychener, Rosie and Amos Yoder, Shirley and Don Fike, the ladies of Lockport and Evangelical Mennonite Church, members of St. Peter's Catholic Church and all the other area churches which donated food and time, those who worked on my beautiful quilt, those who helped plan the community benefit dinner for us, those who donated gifts and clothing for Jeffrey, members of my softball team, and all my fellow teachers and former students who came to see me.

A special thank-you goes to the doctors, nurses, and others working in hospitals where I was a patient, and those medical researchers who dedicate their lives to finding causes and cures for serious illnesses. I believe that God reaches out to us today and performs miracles through the medical profession.

Many others gave their time and their love, expecting nothing in return. Thank you, and may God bless you.

Love, Carol Marchal Storrer

PREFACE

Tom and Carol Storrer have endured more trials and struggles in the first few years of their marriage than most couples encounter in a lifetime. Theirs is a story of love that was tested by years of separation, huge hospital bills, a shattering diagnosis, and heartbreaking setbacks. It's a story of following one's convictions in the face of danger, a story of joy and faith, and a testimony that God works in all things.

This is also a story of the love and concern of Christian people. In an age that is increasingly self-concerned, Carol and Tom found that the care, help, and prayers extended by their Christian friends and neighbors made a tremendous difference in their lives. Committed Christians make the time to help each other, pray for each other, bear each other's burdens, and actively let Christ's love show through their lives, as did the Storrers' family, friends, and neighbors.

Helping to tell Carol's story has been an inspiration. The love and loyalty, the perseverance and prayer have already touched many lives. Why some people are healed but others aren't, in spite of deep faith and fervent prayer, is a mystery only God understands. Yet the Lord has built healing powers into our bodies, and faith and prayer can certainly set that power into motion. Carol and her friends did not ask God to change his natural laws; they asked the Lord to release his power to act within his perfect laws and plan. God clearly states in his Word that he expects us to pray. Carol admits that she was often too sick and weary to pray for herself, but Christian friends always held her up in prayer. Their steadfastness, Carol says, strengthened her. And her ordeal gave her and those around her insight as to how the Lord works.

"We know that all things work together for good to them that love God, to them who are the called according to his purpose" (Rom. 8:28).

VICKI HESTERMAN

INTRODUCTION

I BELIEVE IN MIRACLES . . . and I am one. It's wonderful to be alive. A few years ago, I wouldn't have cared if I were alive or not. Because of love and prayer, I'm still here.

Have you ever stopped to think about all the things most of us take for granted? Walking? Running? Eating? Rolling over in bed? Wiggling your toes or blowing your nose? Probably not. I never used to think about those things, either.

When doctors told me I would probably be permanently quadriplegic, it was more than I was ready to hear. I was only 28 and had high hopes of being a good wife and, perhaps someday, a mother. Neither Tom nor I, nor many of our friends would accept the fact that I would never walk or use my hands again. On several occasions I tried to accept the fact that I would always be dependent on others. But I couldn't. My husband and I decided that we would make the best of things, but never give up hope that I would be normal again, even if it took until I was 99 years old. Then began our long journey that involved doctors, faith, prayer, hospitals, and a lot of love and concern from fellow Christians. My condition was bewildering; even today doctors don't completely agree on the diagnosis.

Why some people are healed and others aren't is a mystery to me. But I know that God is the divine Physician, and he can change any diagnosis.

The only way we made it, and are still making it, is to live each day one by one, trusting God. "I can do all things through Christ which strengtheneth me" (Phil. 4:13).

CAROL MARCHAL STORRER

PROLOGUE

June 1977

SOMETHING TERRIFYING WAS HAPPENING to me. I felt as if I were moving slowly through a nightmare.

"What am I doing here? Oh, dear God, let me wake up beside Tom, at home. Let me be OK," I sobbed as I squeezed my eyes shut against the sight of the sterile white walls.

"What is wrong with me? I should be at home writing thank-you notes and unpacking wedding presents. I can't even pick up a pencil. This can't be happening."

But it was happening. Something was terribly wrong and I had denied it and denied it until I was forced to accept reality. I wanted to call my husband but the phone fell to the floor from my grasp. My body wouldn't cooperate with my brain. I moaned in agony, and finally drifted off into a restless sleep, my mind filled with thoughts of the joyful anticipation that had filled my life only a few weeks before . . .

1

AN OHIO SPRING BREEZE was gently blowing through the trees as I stepped up to bat. I loved softball and was an enthusiastic player.

"Go, Carol! Hit that ball!" I heard my sister's voice call. More of my teammates shouted encouragement.

My fingers were tingling strangely and the bat slipped from my grip. I couldn't seem to hold it, and I struck out. I had also made several catching errors, so I benched myself, disgusted. I was dropping everything lately, it seemed.

"What's wrong, Carol, wedding jitters?" teased one of the girls.

"Probably," I laughed.

"You'll be OK. You're just nervous about the wedding," she reassured me.

I agreed. My hectic life was enough to make anyone a bit nervous. I taught junior high home economics, played on this women's softball team, advised the school cheerleaders, and spent as much time as possible with my fiance, Tom, planning our June wedding.

Tom and I were excited about our future together. We had

known each other for nearly four years, and were friends long before we fell in love. I had dated enough other men to feel confident that Tom and I were right for each other.

Everything would have been perfect if it weren't for my growing clumsiness. A strange weakness in my hands kept getting worse and worse until I couldn't even open cans by myself. Tom noticed it, too, but we both thought I was overtired, and that things would be fine after the wedding.

Several days after the game, Tom's mother, Ruth, and I were planning to shop for a few things for the wedding. I tried to turn on the car ignition, but couldn't. Finally, using both hands to grip the key, I turned it and the car motor roared to life.

Tom's mother watched in silence. Then she asked, "Carol, are you all right?" Concern showed in her face.

"Takes two hands to turn the key—I must really have the jitters," I joked, fighting down an uneasy feeling. "I'm just tired."

There was just too much to do. Working at school, making Ruth's dress and some of the bridesmaids' dresses, and planning the wedding had to be done. But I had always thrived on being busy. My life was filled with people and activity, and I was too excited about my wedding to worry about my weakness.

———◆———

I had begun losing weight early in December. Other teachers at school often commented that I looked pale and tired. I thought I would feel better in the summer, when I could rest. Frankly, I was delighted to be losing weight so effortlessly. My half-hearted attempts to diet had never been very successful, yet I suddenly found myself in a size 8. I just cheerfully took my clothes in and enjoyed my new figure.

Thank the Lord we can't see into the future. Had I known what lay ahead, I don't know if I would have had the strength to bear it. I doubt if I would have gone through with my marriage; I loved Tom too much to knowingly drag him into such an ordeal.

I had always been exceptionally healthy. In fact, in the six years I had taught in the towns of Archbold and Ridgeville Corners, Ohio, I had not missed a single day of school for sickness. When President Ford announced the swine flu vaccine program in the fall of 1976, I debated about taking it, then decided it would probably be a good idea. It seemed everyone was concerned about the flu; I thought I had better be inoculated. I had the shot in November, along with millions of other Americans. Tom was in Thailand on business at the time, so I didn't have a chance to talk it over with him.

Tom had an exciting job traveling around the country and sometimes abroad in sales and service. I missed him so much when he was gone. From one airport or another he would call to tell me he loved me, but so often he was delayed somewhere, or a flight was changed, or something would happen to ruin our plans to be together. When he decided to give up his job and find one closer to home so that we could be married and have a stable life together, I was glad. We both decided it would be the best thing for our marriage. Marriage is tough enough without being separated any more than necessary, and we were well aware of that. Neither of us had been married before, but we had both seen too many failed marriages.

"When I get married, it's for keeps," Tom told me once.

I agreed with him.

Finally, after so much separation, we were going to be together all the time. I couldn't wait to be married to Tom.

Our friends said we seemed made for each other, and I thought so, too. We balance each other. Tom is a man of few words, but what he says counts. I talk to everyone, say what I think as I'm thinking it (which sometimes gets me in hot water!), and I love to visit with people. I think we look like we belong together, too. Although Tom is six feet tall and I'm just 5′ 5″, we're both dark-haired and dark-eyed. My pride and joy for ten years was my shiny, waist-length hair. Tom loved my long hair, too. I enjoyed brushing through all that hair and feeling it blowing in the wind or streaming behind me as I ran outside.

We both came from large farm families. I have six sisters and two brothers, and Tom has five sisters and two brothers.

Tom's parents owned a little house in the country, and it was there we intended to begin our married life. Near a beautiful wooded park and river, and at the end of a long lane, it was a special place—just right for two—where I hoped to spend many happy hours with my husband.

I enjoyed fixing up the house and making plans. I often wished that my mother could have been with me to help. My special day was one she had looked forward to, also. Mom had died of cancer ten years earlier. Her death was sudden and unexpected—she just got sick, Dad drove her to the hospital, and she never came back. My little brother Mike was only five years old at the time. I was 17, and the pain of losing my mother was unbelievably agonizing. Ten years later, it still hurt sometimes, though I was used to the pain. Mom would have loved Tom, I knew, and that thought comforted me.

At last school ended and my wedding day arrived. Last-minute preparations, greeting old friends and relatives, and spending my few precious spare moments with Tom had filled the last few days and hours before the wedding.

We were married in a big Catholic ceremony. Both Tom and I had been raised as Catholics, and we wanted to feel that God would bless our marriage. I had learned all the right words, and I tried to live a good life and be a good example. I didn't pray a lot, except for memorized, group prayers. I saw God as a benevolent figure somewhere "out there" who was responsible for beauty, happiness, and good things. He existed and we existed, and he could head off problems; otherwise there wasn't too much interaction as far as I could tell.

After Mom died, I was angry with God for awhile and refused to pray much, but I got over that. Still, God didn't really figure into my day-to-day life. He was a faraway being. I believed in him, but I planned my own life and got along just fine that way.

Our church wedding went smoothly. My six sisters all had parts in the wedding. The bridesmaids wore long green and white dresses, and Tom's brothers and friends wore tuxedos. My dad, brothers, and other relatives and friends joined Tom's family and friends in celebrating our marriage. When my dad walked me up the aisle and I saw Tom waiting for me, my heart beat harder. All the old cliches of love really are true at a time like that.

I repeated the vows, knowing I intended to honor them forever. Tom and I promised to spend the rest of our lives together, for better or worse. I didn't really expect the "for worse" part to show up for awhile, if ever.

"I now pronounce you man and wife," said Father Alt, and Tom and I hurried down the aisle as Mr. and Mrs. Storrer.

Big tables of food, music, and square dancing were waiting for the guests at our reception. Tom and I joined the fun, but I just couldn't keep a grip on his hand. He had to hold me up several times to prevent me from falling.

I watched Tom, all dressed up in his tuxedo, his eyes shining, talking and laughing with our friends. I decided that my new husband was, without a doubt, the most handsome man there.

Everything was working out just as I had always dreamed it would. I had a good husband, my health, a career I enjoyed, a home, enough money, and plenty of friends. I was content. No wonder I was feeling quite satisfied with God just then.

My carefully-tailored life began to fall apart at the seams on our honeymoon. We drove to Niagara Falls and Canada. It was romantic and a lot of fun, but I became weak whenever we went sightseeing. I fell into bed each night exhausted. Anxiety began to gnaw at me.

"Tom, I'm so weak. I thought I'd have more pep by now," I worried out loud one evening.

"You'll feel better after we get home and you can relax," he reassured me.

On the way home I felt better, but was still jittery and tired. I looked forward to relaxing for a few days and opening our wedding presents when we arrived at home, but one look around our house and yard told me there was a lot of work ahead before we could take it easy.

Some of our friends had played a traditional newlyweds' joke on us and hung paper streamers all over the house. They got inside and created all kinds of mischief. Labels were stripped from all our cans so we had no idea what was in them until we opened them.

"We're going to have some interesting meals, Tom," I had to laugh.

Our bathtub was filled with gelled Jell-O, there was Vaseline on the doorknobs, and our bed was short-sheeted.

We did laugh, but it was an incredible amount of work to make the place livable again. I had a feeling that in his bachelor days Tom had played similar jokes on his newly married friends. My weakness increased as I tried to clean up the mess. Tom was upset because our car had been painted with "Just Married" and "Congratulations" and the shoe polish our well-meaning friends had used wouldn't come off completely. We had washed it numerous times on our honeymoon, and he scrubbed it again as I cleaned up the house.

My plans for a relaxing first day at home didn't materialize. Early that evening I collapsed into bed, exhausted again.

2

My ARMS AND HANDS were undeniably weaker than before the honeymoon, but I told myself all I needed was a good long rest. I slept late the next day, and decided to go grocery shopping in the afternoon. I loved to cook, and was looking forward to making a special supper for Tom.

"I'll ride along to town with you. I need to stop at my folks' place," Tom said before I left.

I dropped him off at his parents' home on the outskirts of town, and drove to a little grocery store. I saw some watermelons in the cooler, and decided to buy one because the day was so hot, and Tom loved watermelon. I found the perfect melon, big and firm, and picked it up. To my shock, I immediately fell to my knees and the melon slipped from my grasp.

"Oh, no," I gasped, closing my eyes against the sure sight of red fruit and black seeds splattering all over the store. Luckily, the fruit landed at a crazy angle in a little wire shopping basket. If I had known how much trouble that watermelon would cause, I would have left it there and gone home.

I was puzzled and embarrassed. As a teen-ager, I had always been proud of the fact that I was a strong farm girl. I had helped my mother milk the cows, and I used to help bale the hay and stack the bales three high. A little watermelon wasn't going to get the best of me. Still, I couldn't quite lift it.

Finally, I managed to get to my feet, hook my fingers through the basket wires, and lug the watermelon to the counter. The clerk gave me a strange look, but I was too embarrassed to explain what had happened. Besides, I wasn't sure I knew.

I didn't want to tell her that I was too weak to carry the watermelon, so I asked her to put it in a box and I hugged it against my chest. The minute I stepped outside the store, I started losing my strength. Visions of my watermelon bursting on Main Street prompted me to set it on the hood of the nearest parked car. I didn't quite know what to do next.

Two boys came walking down the sidewalk toward me. I stopped them: "Would one of you mind carrying this melon to my car? It's just too heavy for me," I smiled.

"Sure, no problem," said the shorter of the two as he effortlessly picked up the melon. "Where's your car?"

"Oh, right here," I sheepishly said, pointing to the car right next to us.

He gave me an incredulous look, shrugged his shoulders, and put the fruit in my car. I drove straight to Tom's parents' house and burst into tears. I blurted out all my fears to Tom.

"Something's really wrong," I sobbed. "I couldn't carry groceries. I couldn't lift a watermelon. I'm always tired. Tom, I'm so scared!"

He hugged me and soothed me, but he didn't know what was wrong, either. We were both scared.

Later, at home, I decided to take a shower. The warm water was soothing and I was feeling a little better.

"Maybe it was just a really heavy watermelon," I started rationalizing.

Then I reached up to shampoo my long hair, and my arms wouldn't work at all. They fell to my sides, too heavy to lift.

"Tom," I yelled, "Come quick."

He ran into the bathroom, fear in his face. Tears were streaming down my cheeks, and I sobbed, "I can't even wash my hair."

He reached in the shower, getting all wet, and washed and rinsed my hair. Then he just held me. We both knew I had to see a doctor, and I had a sinking feeling that I wouldn't be coming right home.

I packed my bags before we went to the doctor's office, because I was sure he would send me directly to the hospital. Tom drove me to the office and waited as the doctor examined me.

I was so scared that I cried all the way through the exam.

"Now, when did your symptoms begin?" he asked after I gripped some objects and my muscle strength was tested.

I told him. Then he asked if I had ever had a swine flu vaccination. I said that I had.

"I think we should have you thoroughly examined in the hospital, Carol," he said. "Go home, get your things, and have Tom drive you there today. I'll make the arrangements." Something in his face said that he knew more than he was telling me.

"I already have everything," I said numbly.

I cried and cried all the way to the hospital. The Fulton County Health Center, a modern hospital only twelve miles from home, was a good hospital, but it seemed so unfair to be going there at all when I was planning to be at home with Tom, unwrapping our wedding gifts.

Still, although I was worried and upset, I had no doubts that everything would be back to normal soon. This was a temporary inconvenience, and the doctors would give me some medicine to fix me up like new.

I was checked in and within an hour found myself in a hospital bed, only nine days after I had marched down the church aisle with Tom. He was as upset as I was. He stayed with me as long as he could, and tried to reassure me. I cried myself to sleep that night.

The next few days were a blur of tests—blood tests, reflex tests, grip tests, X-rays, and a spinal tap. Some didn't hurt a bit, but others were pretty painful. The spinal tap made me nervous and gave me severe headaches for several days afterward.

I took a pulmonary breathing test that was designed to determine if I was breathing normally. I had to press my lips tightly against a tube hooked to a machine and take first a normal breath, then the deepest breath possible.

"OK, Carol, drink this," one of the technicians told me.

I swallowed what looked like a strawberry milkshake. It definitely was not a milkshake; the liquid had barium in it, and I thought I would vomit before I finished it. After I drank the chalky mixture, I was X-rayed.

Still another test involved inserting a tube through my nose, down my throat, and into my stomach to draw out some of the stomach contents. The nurse who pushed the tube down my throat had been my student several years earlier. In school, she always had to follow my instructions. Now the tables were turned.

"Swallow, swallow," she urged as the tube passed through my throat.

I wanted to gag and choke; it was a terrible sensation.

The respiratory therapist then drew blood from an artery in my wrist to find out what my blood gases were. I thought it might hurt a little, but I had no idea that arteries are much deeper than veins.

"This might hurt a little, Carol," he said.

"Oh, that's OK, I can take it," I told him, confident that a little pin-pricking wouldn't bother me.

I was sitting up when he began to stick me. Then the room started spinning and I became dizzy and almost fainted. For the first time in my life, I had to be revived with smelling salts. No wonder people come back to their senses. The odor was awful.

Several times I was asked if I had ever had a swine flu shot. When I replied that I had, no one seemed surprised.

"Why, is this connected to that shot?" I asked. "Is it a reaction or something?"

No one seemed to know for sure.

After the doctors had completed their tests, they told me that I had Guillain-Barré Syndrome, a disease that I had never heard of and couldn't even pronounce, much less spell. I kept forgetting the name of it and finally asked a nurse to write it down so I could tell my family what was wrong with me.

Much later, this diagnosis would be questioned, but at the time everyone seemed certain that Guillain-Barré Syndrome was causing my problems. In a way, I was relieved that my condition had a name.

"At least it's not something really terrible," I told Tom.

Because I didn't understand how serious Guillain-Barré Syndrome (or GBS, as we all called it) was, I assumed that the doctors could stop the disease right away. I had high hopes of leaving the hospital in a few days, completely recovered.

The more I learned about GBS, though, the more frightened I became. It can be a devastating disease that completely paralyzes its victims. GBS is a rare illness that destroys the linings of the nerves and causes progressive muscle weakness. People can die from GBS, although many do recover most of their strength eventually. Most medical experts agree that it's an abnormal immune response. Somehow my immune system was going crazy. Instead of attacking foreign antibodies, my system was attacking the myelin sheath (fatty protein) protecting my nerve fibers. Sporadic nerve sheath deterioration and weakness was the result. GBS made my nerves act like wires that won't conduct electricity.

No one could forecast how long I would be sick, or how helpless I would become. My doctors had never seen a case in our community. I had never heard of anyone having GBS.

"Why me?" I wondered in tears. "Why now?"

I had never really been sick before, except for a few colds and the normal childhood illnesses. To be confined to a small hospital room, alone and frightened, with such a diagnosis, was devastating.

My doctors tried all kinds of medication, including a steroid, to try to control the disease. Despite that, I couldn't grip anything. My arms and hands were getting weaker daily. I couldn't put on makeup, wash or brush my hair, or bathe. Everything had to be done for me. For an independent 27-year-old, this was hard to take.

I turned 28 while in the hospital. July 3 had always been a big celebration day for me, but this year I was in no mood to party. Tom and some of my friends came and tried to cheer me up, but I wasn't much fun.

One morning, two weeks after I had been admitted, I swung my legs over the bed, as I had done so many times before. I took two or three steps and fell to the floor. Totally baffled and frightened, I screamed for a nurse. She came running and helped me back to bed. Sobbing, I lay back in bed, afraid to try to move. My legs had been getting weaker, but I didn't realize the disease would affect my legs as well as my arms. If anyone had told me that, I had blocked it out.

I cried on and off that entire day. For the first time in my life, I had to use a bedpan. I was absolutely humiliated. I remembered how my grandmother had to use a bedpan during the last years of her life, and I thought it was so awful. I never dreamed I would be using one at the age of 28.

The same day I also had to be fed by the nurses because my arms had grown so weak. I choked down the little food I ate that day, sobbing through each mouthful. I felt so helpless and out of control. As a home economics teacher for the previous six years, I had taught hundreds of young girls to sew and cook and groom themselves. Now I couldn't even feed myself or go to the bathroom alone.

I felt good and sorry for myself. I had never considered the possibility that self-sufficient Carol would ever need to be so dependent on others for basic necessities. Yet here I was, needing the nurses' help for everything.

The nurses had weighed me every day since I began the

steroids. I always walked to the scales with no difficulty. Now, with one nurse on each side of me, I slowly shuffled out to the hallway to the scales. It was a tedious, time-consuming process. Every time the nurses helped me walk, fear of falling overtook me.

"Tom, Tom, why is this happening to me?" I cried when he came to visit.

He had no answers, but just having him there was a big help. When he and I were married, I had visions of the two of us living "happily ever after" as in the fairy tales I'd read as a child. We were very much in love, and I had high expectations of my marriage. These did not include the painful struggle of battling a rare and incapacitating disease.

My family, friends, and fellow teachers came to visit me often, which was encouraging. I worried so much about how I looked, though, that sometimes I didn't enjoy my company as much as I should have. I wasn't used to having people see me at anything less than my best. I hated being seen in a hospital gown with unkempt hair.

Anxiety gnawed at me. I was afraid I wouldn't get better in time to teach school in the fall. I began having terrible thoughts that Tom would leave me for a normal woman. I feared that I would be one of the small percentage of GBS victims who would end up paralyzed or dead.

Despite my fears, though, I still had a deep-down confidence that the doctors would "fix" me eventually and I could go home. I couldn't imagine staying in bed very long.

As the long days passed, my appetite grew voracious. I ate everything and wanted more, yet I lost weight and was soon down to 106 pounds. When I looked in the mirror, I was horrified. Several weeks earlier I had been a radiant bride and now I looked like Frankenstein's bride! The medication had left me with a rounded, grotesque moonface and a big, bloated stomach. I wanted to hide from the world.

Insomnia was another upsetting side effect. I was lucky if I slept four or five hours a night. The nurses were quite concerned about me, and checked on me often. They kept my door partially open so they could hear me if I called, and the hall noises and activity bothered me. When a nurse came in to check me with her flashlight, my usual reply was a half-cynical "Yes, I'm still alive."

I resented being in the hospital. It didn't matter which hospital it was, or how good the care was, I didn't want to be there. I wanted to be at home with Tom.

My appetite doubled, and then tripled. If I didn't eat a lot, I got sick to my stomach. The first time I woke up in the middle of the night feeling hungry, I could have eaten a steak dinner. The kitchen was closed at that hour, so I clumsily rummaged around and attacked a plate of homemade cookies from Tom's mom. I gobbled down six in a row. Other nights when I awoke, I ate whatever I could find, cookies or candy, to quiet down my growling stomach so I could get some sleep.

At first I felt lucky to be able to eat and eat without gaining an ounce. Then my home economics training caught up with me and I began to wonder what the medication might be doing to my body. Since it was burning so many calories, I was afraid that it might also be destroying important vitamins and minerals. I could see myself getting weaker and weaker, and was convinced that vitamins would help.

I told my doctors that I wanted to take vitamins, and we disagreed about how useful they would be. I insisted on being allowed to take them. Dr. Thompson took over my case as my full-time doctor, and didn't really think vitamins would help much either, but at least he let me take them. I felt so much better, knowing that if the medication was destroying essential nutrients, at least I was putting some extra ones back into my body.

My days were filled with hospital routine—physical therapy twice a day, sponge baths given me by the nurses, meals and snacks. Visitors helped to brighten up the day. I watched a lot of television because I couldn't hold a book or newspaper and couldn't grip a pen to write.

I often felt as if I were in a nightmare.

"What am I doing here? Oh, dear God, please let me wake up beside Tom at home. Let me be OK," I cried myself to sleep more than once.

I wanted to be at home writing my thank-you notes. I wanted to call Tom and talk to him, but the phone fell to the floor from my grasp. My body wouldn't cooperate with my brain. Time and again I would drift off into sleep, remembering the joyful anticipation that had filled my life such a short time ago.

But when I awoke, things were always the same. Trying to do simple, everyday things was terribly frustrating.

Tom came every day. He was handling the situation incredibly well. Maybe he was just acting for my sake, but whenever he came to see me, he was strong and calm. We would talk, watch television, or play chess. I was pretty clumsy, and couldn't pick up the pieces very well.

"You win because by the time I have a piece moved, I forgot what I was doing," I told him. He just laughed.

I wanted so much to look pretty for Tom. I don't think I was being vain; I was a new bride, and naturally I wanted to look attractive for my husband. But whenever I looked in a mirror, I saw a chipmunk staring back. Sometimes I would cry because I couldn't believe that the reflection in the mirror could possibly be me.

"Carol, stop it. You look fine," Tom often said.

I thought that I looked grotesque and was sure he was just being polite. Poor Tom. I'm sure he had no idea he would be in for this. Neither of us ever expected the vows "for better or worse" to test our love so soon.

Tom's sister Diane came to the hospital twice a week to wash and dry my hair. Because it was so long, it got quite snarled. She knew how much it meant to me to have my hair look nice, and long hair like mine was a bother to care for. No one seriously suggested that I cut it short, and I wouldn't have listened if they had. My long hair was part of me. I wanted to keep as much of my life as normal as possible, especially until I was walking again.

After several weeks, I began slowly to regain strength in my arms and legs. My muscles gradually grew stronger and I was able to move my arms and legs around in bed, then lift weights with them, and finally, to walk with the help of only one nurse.

Whether the disease had run its course or the physical therapy and medicine were responsible for my improvements, we weren't sure. But I was delighted at my progress.

Often as I struggled to feed myself, more hit the tray than went into my mouth. I was so messy. The nurses tucked a towel inside the neckline of my gown, bib-like. Getting the food on my fork or spoon took a lot of effort, and often by the time I got the spoon to my mouth, the food had already spilled down the front of me and into my lap.

One evening, meatballs were on the menu. Tom was visiting me, and I wanted to show off that I was getting stronger.

"Watch me, Tom, I'm eating pretty well now," I told him, as I stabbed the entire meatball and lifted it toward my mouth. I was so proud that I could lift an entire meatball all by myself. Just as I was about to take a bite, the weight of the meatball became too much for me to hold up, and it fell to the floor with a plop.

Tom solemnly bent over, picked up the meatball, wiped it off and gave it back to me. After all that work, I ate it.

Physical therapy was strenuous and tiring, but I knew it was helping. The therapists helped me exercise my arms and legs for 5½ days a week. I could feel myself getting stronger, and worked extra hard so I could go home soon.

"Carol, put on your tennis shoes," my therapist said one day. Others had been doing this for me for weeks.

"Oh, I don't think I can yet," I protested.

"Just try it," he urged.

I gave it my best try, but it was difficult and frustrating to swing my leg up high enough to cross it so I could put the shoe on and tie the lace. My knees didn't want to bend. I was shocked that my muscles had tightened up so much in the short time I had been hospitalized.

Sometimes my legs felt like rubber bands that would snap or tear under pressure. Using the muscles exhausted me.

"You'll have to work at flexibility, Carol. It's important to keep your muscles from tightening up," he added. "Have others move your arms and legs for you if you can't do it."

I was amazed at how much work it was just to regain flexibility. I guess I had taken each day of my life for granted before I got sick. I never thought much about sick or handicapped people before. I took for granted going to the bathroom by myself, feeding myself, bathing myself, and walking alone. I never thought I would fall victim to a severe illness. Things like that happened to other unfortunate people, but not to me. Wrong!

As I did my exercises, I longed to be at home with Tom, cooking for him, cleaning our little house, sewing, doing the laundry, and just being there. I felt terribly guilty about the whole situation.

"Stop it. You couldn't help it," he said when I tried to apologize. I wanted to give him a big hug but my arms still weren't working well enough.

"Carol, want to go home for a little visit?" Tom asked one day with a big grin on his face. He knew what my answer would be.

"Really, Tom? I'd love it!" I beamed.

I had been in the hospital for a month, and my doctor encouraged Tom to take me home for a few hours to see how I would do. If everything went all right, and I continued to improve, I might be dismissed soon.

Tom came to get me the next Sunday afternoon. I had been anticipating that day since the minute I knew I could go home.

He lifted me from the wheelchair into our car, and we were off.

The ride through the country to our house was thrilling; my heart was pounding because I was so excited.

The grass was bright green, the temperature typically July-hot, and the corn had grown tall while I was gone. I felt as though I were seeing the farms and trees and fields for the first time. I realized I had never really looked at it all before.

When we arrived at our house, Tom carried me from the car up our porch steps and into our home. Our simple little house looked brand new to me. Our furniture consisted of a broken-down couch that we covered with a blanket, a rocker, and a TV set. We had been planning to buy some nice living room furniture after the honeymoon, but I had ended up in the hospital instead.

Tom had cleaned the entire house and everything looked spotless. I was quite impressed.

He had set up a lawn chair in the living room for me to sit in, because it had arms on the side that I could hold onto as I sat. I couldn't walk around from room to room, but it was wonderful to be back in familiar surroundings once again. It was a pleasant but modest home, and that was fine with us.

"Oh, Tom, I miss being home. I miss you so much I can hardly stand it," I told him.

"I really miss you too," he said, and gave me a hug and a big kiss.

The afternoon flew by. Mostly I just sat in my lawn chair, looking around, remembering many special moments we had shared there. I was so grateful to Tom for taking the time and making the effort to create such a pleasant afternoon for me. My dad surprised us by dropping in to visit. Dad lived 100 miles away, so it was a long trip for him. The nurses had told him I was at home for the afternoon.

I was completely exhausted by the time we returned, but happy. Now I wanted more than ever to recover and go home again.

3

WALKING AND LIVING AT HOME like a normal person were my goals. I was willing to work hard to regain my abilities, but often wondered why God had let me get into such a fix in the first place.

"Maybe it's so I'll appreciate little things, and be a better person," I decided.

My sister Margie, a dedicated Christian, came to visit, and we talked about why I was so sick. Margie and her family lived in the Virgin Islands, but had not yet gone home after my wedding. I loved Margie dearly, but was puzzled by how excited she was about her faith. She kept talking about how the Lord fills us with his Spirit and works actively in our lives. I thought she went a bit overboard on the faith bit. In fact, I considered her a religious fanatic.

"Carol, can I lay hands on you and pray for your healing?" she asked.

I lay there in that hospital bed, too desperate to be walking again to care about the fact that I had never considered that sort of thing my style. I agreed to let my sister pray for me.

She came to my bedside, placed her hands on me, and prayed, claiming my healing.

"Jesus, we just ask you to heal Carol. Come into her heart and be alive to her. We claim your promises of healing. . . ."

I didn't really expect anything, but deep down there was an unreasonable hope that maybe her prayer would do the trick and I would be miraculously healed and leap out of that bed. I wasn't and didn't.

"The Lord is with you, Carol, and we'll all be praying for you. Remember that," she encouraged me as she left. "And remember Romans 8:28, that all things do work together for good to them that love the Lord."

I really wanted to believe what she said. But I just couldn't see how my sickness could be good for anyone or anything.

I did pray quite a bit. But I never asked the Lord to be in charge of my life. I just wanted God to make me better so I could get out of that hospital bed and on my feet again.

The love and concern from my family, teachers, and friends from Archbold and Ridgeville, and even people I scarcely knew kept my spirits up. People from my church, St. Peter's, came to visit. Many of my visitors told me they were praying for Tom and me. Although I was praying, too, I still worried constantly, but I tried to act cheerful and optimistic around visitors.

As my steroid dosage decreased and then was ended, the terrible insomnia and insatiable appetite subsided. In physical therapy I slowly learned to walk a little on crutches, but someone had to help me because I tended to lose my balance. Forty-seven days after I was admitted, I was discharged from the hospital. I was ecstatic.

Tom picked me up, loaded my things and me into the car, and we left the hospital. Although we couldn't wait to get home and begin our life together, we both knew that I was more work than Tom could handle alone. I still couldn't bathe, dress, wash my hair, cook, or do much of anything except walk a little on crutches and exercise with weights.

My sister Pat and her husband Rich lived only a few miles from us and invited Tom and me to stay with them until I was stronger. We gratefully accepted their offer, and went directly to their home from the hospital.

Since I could barely use my crutches on ground level, managing the three steps into their house was impossible. Strong and muscular Tom just picked me up easily and carried me in.

Tom and Pat helped me do all the things the nurses and therapists did for me in the hospital. We all realized then how difficult it is to care for someone as helpless as I was. I found myself missing some of the nurses and therapists I had grown close to. They were good to me, and because they were paid to take care of me, I didn't feel as badly about asking them for help as I did constantly bothering Pat or Tom. The nurses worked in 8-hour shifts, but Pat and Tom had to put up with my needs 24 hours a day. They were good, but sometimes I heard a sigh or saw a look of impatience cross their faces, and I felt like a burden.

In the mornings, Tom would dress me and help me walk out to the kitchen. Pat cooked nutritious meals for us and I continued to gain strength.

Pat helped me do so many things, even brush my teeth. The first time, I wanted to brush them in the kitchen, sitting at the table. The nurses always let me brush at my bedside table, I told my sister.

"No, Carol, let's go to the bathroom and brush like you always did at home. Come on, I'll walk with you," Pat insisted.

"Pat, I'll fall. I'm scared," I told her. As much as I wanted to be normal, I still wanted to do it at my own pace.

Determined that I would do things like a normal person, Pat walked me to the bathroom. I held the toothbrush with both hands, but couldn't get the cap off the toothpaste to squeeze the paste onto my brush. Pat helped again. Then I was afraid that I would fall, because I needed both hands to move the brush around in my mouth. That meant that I had no free hand to hold onto the sink to keep me from losing my balance and falling. Somehow I managed.

After that ordeal was over, I felt I had really accomplished something. My first hurdle had been passed.

Pat kept urging me to do things normally. Sometimes I resisted her pushing, but she helped me overcome my fears and recover faster.

"Let me alone," I snapped more than once at Pat's insistence that I push myself more than I thought I should. I had grown used to being taken care of in the hospital, and while I wanted to go home, I had a tremendous fear of falling which was holding me back from doing some things.

Pat kept right on encouraging me, pushing me, and insisting that I not baby myself. She went out of her way to help us in so many ways. We needed weights so that I could do my physical therapy at home, so Pat got some material, sand, and Velcro fasteners and made them for me. We fastened the handmade weights to my wrists and ankles, and they worked just fine as I exercised strength back into my weak and wasted muscles.

Pat also often dressed me, shampooed and combed my hair, and cooked for us. She lost her patience sometimes, and I didn't blame her. Caring for me was like taking care of a great big baby. Sometimes I acted like one, too.

Twice a week, Tom drove me back to the hospital for therapy. Dr. Thompson kept close tabs on my progress, and was pleased that I was getting better. Two weeks after I had been discharged from the hospital, I felt strong enough to try living at home.

When the day I had been looking forward to for two months finally arrived, I drank in the sights and smells of the familiar countryside as we drove from Pat's house to ours. Our little place looked better to me than a mansion on a hill. I was home at last—this time to stay. I looked up at Tom and smiled. He had seemed a lot less worried lately. His face had relaxed and he laughed more easily. I was glad, because I knew that this had been a terrible strain on him. He had kept it all inside.

Theresa, the youngest of my six sisters, offered to stay with us until her classes at Ohio State University began in mid-September. Theresa has a zany sense of humor, and did her best to dispel any depression or irritable spells that ever started to come over me. I thoroughly enjoyed her cheerful spirit.

"Hey, Tarzan and Jane," she declared the first time she saw Tom carrying me. From then on, we were Tarzan and Jane and she became Mabel the Maid because she was cooking and cleaning for us.

I kept on improving during Theresa's stay with us. Every day I could do a little bit more. Each improvement was a source of celebration. Silly and sensitive, Theresa kept us laughing as she helped me. Her attitude helped me laugh at things again.

By the time she had to leave for college, I could dress and do some other basic things for myself. As much as we loved having Theresa around, it was good to have some privacy at last, after 2½ months of constantly being with other people.

For the first time since early July, I was dressing myself alone. Brushing my hair was such a joy; I hadn't had the strength to lift my arms and run a brush through my hair for so long.

I could even cook a little, although my legs hurt if I stood more than a few minutes without something to lean my weight on. Even the simple meals I prepared for us tasted like gourmet dishes to me.

"Do you like this, honey?" I asked Tom as he wolfed down a chicken dinner I made one evening.

"MMMph, yeah, great." He must have liked it; he ate enough of it.

Tom was always there when I needed him. He helped me as much as he could, took me to the doctor, buttoned the buttons I couldn't get, and did all the things that were still too hard for me. I couldn't get along without him.

"Tom, thanks," I said one evening as we sat in the living room. He was watching a football game on television. I looked at my husband of less than three months, relaxed on the couch, dressed in old blue jeans and a plaid flannel shirt. I felt so content and loving that I couldn't help hugging him.

"For what?" he asked, looking up from his game.

"For always being around when I need you. For being such a good husband," I said. "For not getting mad at me for getting sick."

"Aw, that's OK. I told you before, you couldn't help it." He went back to watching his football game.

He was so strong and calm, and just took things in stride. I admired him so much. I felt in my heart that God had given me such a steady man to help me through my troubles. I promised myself that I would make it all up to him someday by being a good wife and mother.

I thought about how we met, and I had to laugh. I had been teaching at Archbold Middle School in Ridgeville, only a few miles from Tom's hometown of Archbold. I was 24, and had been dating several of the local available young men, but hadn't found anyone special. Then one night Tom called and asked me for a date. I had had terrible luck with blind dates in the past, so I refused.

"I weigh 300 pounds and I'm 5′ 2″," I teased him. "And I never go out with someone I haven't met."

He didn't push the issue, so we said good-bye and I didn't think much more about it until a few weeks later. I had a date and noticed a tall, dark-haired, good-looking man talking and laughing with some of my friends at a party. He seemed very nice.

Then introductions were made, and I blushed. The handsome man was the same Tom Storrer I had refused to go out with. I couldn't believe it. Tom seemed so nice, and my friends apparently liked him. I was sorry I had given him such a hard time.

He came over later and said hello.

"Funny, you don't look like you weigh 300 pounds," he commented, and I blushed even more.

Later, he told me that he had noticed me in church and already knew a few things about me before he called.

That was the beginning of a friendship, many phone calls across the country as he traveled, and, nearly four years after we met, plans to marry. I really loved Tom, and was glad when he decided to work near home.

I knew that he often missed the excitement of his traveling job, but I intended to make it up to him by doing all I could to make our marriage a good one. Then this strange sickness had to strike.

Sometimes I thought about how devastating it was to spend the first several months of my married life in the hospital, but then I realized that it could have been worse. The hospital was only twelve miles from home, and Tom came to see me every day. I was getting much better, and the doctors said my disease should never return. Once you improved, you had it licked, apparently. I believed them, but once in awhile I had to fight down a nagging fear: What if it did come back?

Despite my fears, we were pretty happy. Tom seemed to be enjoying life, we had a lot of laughs, and were able to keep a sense of humor about most of my problems. I was still awkward and became tired easily.

By the end of September I had graduated from crutches to a cane, and was able to lift 15 pounds with each leg and 13 pounds using both arms. I stopped using my cane in early October, and developed my own special walk. I was slow, and it was sort of a duck-walk, but I was walking alone. What a feeling of triumph! I had overcome the disease, was home again, walking, sewing, cooking, and even washing clothes.

Our washer and dryer were in the basement, and the only way I could get there was by putting a basketful of dirty clothes on my lap, sitting on the top step, and scooting down the stairs. To go back up, I would reverse the process. It was slow, and took hours to do the wash, but I didn't mind. I was just glad to be able to do my own laundry.

We began to make plans for the future. Tom wanted to work hard and buy our own home someday. We both wanted children eventually, when I was completely well. I also intended to go back to my teaching job as soon as possible.

I tried to go outside for a walk every day and soak up the beauty of the country around me. I wanted to fill my mind with the sights and sounds of the wind rushing through the trees, the sun setting orange behind the woods, the birds, the autumn leaves, and the nearby river. Maybe I hadn't ever really noticed it all before. As a teacher, I always had so many things going on that I ran here and there and never took the time to notice the little miracles all around me. When I was barely able to walk and forced to slow down, I found it much easier to appreciate what I once took for granted.

Life was good. When I first came home at the end of August, there was still the humiliation of needing someone to bathe and dress me. Now I took care of those personal things myself.

Tom was so patient and supportive. He rarely criticized me. He hardly ever talked about my sickness, but seemed to accept it and helped me as much as he could. I needed him for his physical strength as well as his emotional strength. At first I had to be carried a lot up and down steps.

I could write again, and finally finished my thank-you notes for our wedding gifts. I even drove my car several times, and the doctors considered me completely functional in my home. I wasn't teaching, but hoped to be able to return to my job in January. The school staff had been good to me, and promised to do as much as possible with sick leave, insurance, and holding my job for me. I was grateful, because I really wanted to teach again. I missed the students and the other teachers.

One day Chris Hammer Korhn, my friend and fellow teacher, came by to take me on a visit to my school. I was looking forward to the visit, and wanted to look nice. I had hoped to be able to wear regular shoes, but was still too unsteady on my feet. I had to wear my trusty old tennis shoes.

Although it was really great to see all my teacher friends again, I felt strange. After teaching at Archbold Middle School every day for four years, I was an outsider, no longer directly involved with the school. When I slowly climbed the stairway I used to scurry up to reach my home economics classroom, I couldn't help but feel a sadness that it was no longer my room.

I clung to the fact that I would be coming back in January as I looked around the school. My fellow teachers greeted me with such delight during my visit that it nearly made up for my self-consciousness about my duck-walk and tennis shoes.

"Carol, you're looking great. Soon you'll be back working for a living like the rest of us!" my principal, Dave Rex, said as he greeted me with a smile. He and his wife Sharon had been regular visitors at the hospital, and were a real encouragement to me. They made me feel like a valuable part of the school. I tried to tell Dave how much his concern meant to me.

Dave gently brushed aside the appreciation.

"Just get yourself better so you can come back," he said.

We had an especially close-knit bunch at my school, an older but comfortable brick building in Ridgeville.

The other teachers had become part of my life, and I really missed them. We enjoyed each other and cared about each other. I wanted to be part of that team again. We teachers grew close as we worked with the same students and tried to guide them as they learned, grew, and overcame problems.

I felt resentment welling up inside me. Not only had the stupid disease robbed me of precious time with Tom, it had cost me months of teaching.

After school was dismissed for the day, I judged cheerleading tryouts. I had been advisor for the junior high football and basketball cheerleaders for the past four years.

I felt inadequate as I judged the girls, because every one of them could do far more physically than I could do, no matter how awkwardly they jumped. I shuffled along, slowly, carefully,

39

and duck-like. These agile girls could run, jump, turn cart-wheels, and clap.

"So could I, not so long ago," I thought sadly.

Even though I wasn't working or walking normally yet, I was happy to be somewhat independent again. One day, as I was outside in the autumn sunshine, I felt so exuberant and optimistic that I tried to run down our lane toward the trees. I immediately fell to the ground. My muscles just weren't strong enough yet. That taught me to be more sensible about my recovery.

Tom hadn't worked since I had gotten sick. He had left his traveling job before the wedding, and intended to start work again after our honeymoon. When I got so sick, all our plans were put on hold. We were both concerned about our financial situation, and when I was finally able to care for myself, Tom went back to work at a large food production plant in town, La Choy's.

Things were working out. I was getting better, Tom had a job, and I was sure I would be back at work in January. I began to make plans for the Thanksgiving and Christmas holidays. To thank my friends and family for all their help and concern, I wanted to prepare a nice meal.

"Tom, what shall we have?" I asked him one evening.

"You're the home ec. teacher. Cook some of the things you used to make. I like it all," was his helpful reply.

I looked forward to the Thanksgiving season with special reason. I had a lot to be thankful for.

Then one cold morning in late October, I noticed that my fingers were numb and tingling. I fought down panic. The battle was behind me, I was sure. Hadn't my doctors said we had won?

Actually, the battle had barely begun.

4

AT FIRST I DENIED that I could be getting worse again. But when I began dropping things and having trouble walking, I knew I was having a relapse.

"It can't come back. The doctors said it was over," I told myself.

Then I began stumbling. One day I tried to walk to the kitchen, and I fell against the wall. Crying in frustration and fear, I began using my cane again. I knew something was terribly wrong inside my body.

"Tom, it's coming back," I said when he got home that night.

"What is?" he asked, a look of apprehension on his face.

"The GBS. I can't walk very well, and I'm getting weaker." I started to cry again.

"No, you're not. It's all in your head, because you're just afraid it will come back. You're better. The doctors said it doesn't come back," he said firmly. I think he was afraid, too.

My family didn't want to believe that I was getting worse again. They thought I was just overdoing things and tiring myself out. I knew better. It was discouraging to watch my hard-earned abilities slipping away, one by one.

I didn't want to be hospitalized again until it was absolutely necessary. Because I was so clumsy and weak, though, I couldn't take very good care of myself. I spent a lot of time at Tom's parents' house while he was at work.

Tom's mother owns a small beauty salon by their home. We both knew, as I struggled with my long hair every day, that I just couldn't take care of it anymore.

I didn't want to cut my hair. It had been long for years.

Finally, after an especially frustrating day of tangling with three feet of hair, I realized that it was just too much work for me. I couldn't expect other people to take the time to care for it.

Tom's mom cut it to my shoulders. I couldn't watch the long ribbons of dark hair fall to the floor. I felt sick inside. Losing my hair was like losing a part of me, a part of my femininity.

"First this disease makes me be separated from Tom. Then I have to give up my job for awhile. Now my hair. It's just NOT FAIR!" I complained, to no one in particular.

During this discouraging time, Charlene Lantz, a woman from Archbold who often had her hair done in Ruth's salon, phoned me. She had heard about my problems, and because I had taught all three of her daughters, she wanted to talk with me.

She seemed a bit nervous as she told me who she was, and that she felt the Lord wanted her to call me and tell me how he had helped her overcome a serious illness.

"Sometime, Carol, I would like to share some Scripture with you, and tell you more about how Jesus healed me," she said, "if you have some time."

"Could you come over this afternoon?" I found myself asking her.

She seemed surprised that I was so eager to hear what she had to say, but was delighted at my curiosity.

"I'll be there!" she promised.

Charlene, a pretty, petite brunette in her late forties, came into my house with a Bible in her hand.

"Carol, I know we don't know each other, but I feel like I

42

know you through my girls," she said with a smile. "My daughter told me how sick you were." She seemed a little bit hesitant, but plunged ahead. "This may seem unusual, but my husband Bob and I have really been praying for you. You've been in our hearts a lot lately. I just felt that the Lord wanted me to share some things with you."

That day, as I fought despair, Charlene shared some of God's promises with me. She was a dedicated Christian, and she assured me that God's Word promises healing and life. I had never read the Bible very much. There were always several Bibles lying around our house as I grew up, but I never took the time to open one and read it.

I was excited to hear that Jesus is the same yesterday, today, and forever, and that God wanted to heal me. I was also skeptical. I didn't want to get my hopes too high. My high hopes hadn't gotten me too far. I really wanted to believe the promises of healing and salvation. But how could God want me to be healthy when I was getting weaker and weaker each day?

Charlene prayed with me before she left.

"Carol, don't give up. The Lord loves you and wants what's best for you. I know he will heal you," she assured me.

"I hope so, but we'll see," I thought.

During the second week of November, my arms were so rubbery that I couldn't cook or pour milk from a bottle. Tom poured a bowl of cereal for me before he went to work. As soon as he left, I put my head in the bowl and ate like an animal. I couldn't even grip silverware anymore. I was so afraid of falling that I would crawl around the house.

Finally, Tom realized what I knew but was trying to deny. I had to go back to the doctor.

"Why? Why would God allow this to happen again?" I cried over and over.

Tom drove me to the doctor, who was baffled to see me going downhill so rapidly.

After he examined me, he made arrangements to admit me to a larger hospital that had a neurological unit.

I could tell that Dr. Thompson was disturbed that my disease had returned. I was fighting off panic, and the tears kept coming.

"Go on back home, and try to relax for a few days, until you go to the hospital," the doctor advised.

Tom and I returned home, to wait for another painful separation. I crawled around the house, because my legs were so weak I couldn't walk unless I had help. My knees were raw and sore by the time we were ready to leave.

The night before I left, Tom carried me down to the basement where our shower is. He sat me on a folding chair, gave me a shower, shampooed my hair, wrapped me in a big towel, and carried me back upstairs. Then he dressed me for bed and combed the tangles out of my hair. He was so strong, both physically and emotionally. I was crying softly all the while.

Tom took off work the next day to help me pack and dress. Just as we were leaving, our neighbor, Mary Ellen Stuckey, stopped to visit.

"Hi! Where are you two going?" she asked, surprised to see my suitcase.

When I tearfully told her I was going back into the hospital, she was shocked. Most of our friends had no idea how rapidly I had regressed. Only several weeks earlier I had been walking and driving.

I took a long look around our house before we left. A feeling of deep sadness came over me. I was also angry. Why was God letting this happen to us? I didn't think I deserved so much trouble. I looked back at the small gray house, and knew it would be some time before I could come home again.

We arrived at the hospital in mid-afternoon. It was about an hour from our home, but since the other hospital had been just twelve miles away, this seemed so much farther. We weren't sure where to park, and since it was a bitterly cold November day we didn't want to walk far. Tom finally found a nearby parking garage, and I held his arm tightly as we crossed the street. Wind whipped my hair into my face, making it difficult to see. My balance was poor, my legs were weakening, and we barely made it into the hospital. By the time we stumbled inside, I was completely exhausted.

"I'll find a wheelchair," Tom said, leading me to a chair in the lobby.

He found a wheelchair and pushed me down the hall to the admittance area. My overnight bag was on my lap. Tom told the receptionist that they were expecting us. She looked at the two of us, smiled, then gave us directions to one of the floors. As we were going down the hallway, I saw pictures of children's storybook characters on the wall, and asked the nurse, "Are you sure we're on the right floor?"

"Oh, yes," she said. "You're expecting, aren't you?"

"Oh, I wish I were. If only that were my problem," I told her.

After we straightened things out, I was taken to the neurological floor and put in a room far from the nurses' station. Once the doctors realized how serious my diagnosis was, they moved me closer to the station.

By the next day, my arms were nearly useless, and they dangled limp and rubber-like, with no strength left. I couldn't lift them at all.

The doctors ran a lot of tests during those first few days. I had an EMG, a spinal tap, and other tests. Some were painful.

"Carol, you have a rare strain of Guillain-Barré Syndrome called recurring GBS," one of my doctors said. "That means you are susceptible to relapses."

"Relapses? How many? You mean this will happen to me again?" I nearly screamed.

I was told the relapses can happen more than once. The victim can struggle to improve, only to get worse again. Sometimes, I found later, the patient dies of respiratory failure because of the paralysis.

"How did I get this? Why me?" I begged the doctors to tell me how I got such a terrible sickness.

They didn't know, but they asked me if I had ever had the swine flu shot. I said yes, and asked again if there was a connection.

"We don't know, Carol," said one doctor. "There may be a connection, but we don't know for sure."

Another doctor said it could have been caused by a virus weakening my system. Someone else heard it could be caused by eating unwashed fruits or vegetables. No one seemed to know for sure what caused it. They did know that it caused my body's defense system to malfunction, and the linings of my nerves were being destroyed. Just as they seemed to be getting better, the disease came back and damaged them again.

I spent most of my time resting in bed, and had to wear pressurized stockings to prevent blood clotting. Switching from sheer nylon stockings and stylish skirts to a hospital gown and pressurized hose was quite a change.

I had a lot of free time during those first few weeks in the hospital, and just enough strength in my arms to hold a book. It was difficult to turn pages, but I managed. One of Kathryn Kuhlman's books described stories of different people who had been miraculously healed. My sister Margie had given me the book, but I never took time to read it before.

I wanted desperately to be well, and I was willing to try nearly anything. Kathryn Kuhlman's book started me thinking. If the people in the book really experienced miracles, why couldn't I? I didn't care how God worked or through whom, just so I got better again.

Linda was a friendly and concerned nurse who took a special interest in me from the beginning. A Christian, Linda had a concern for both my physical and spiritual healing. She often requested me for her patient and we grew very close. I always felt comfortable when Linda was nearby.

Charlene and Bob began coming to visit me every Friday night. I was so surprised that a couple who didn't even know me would take the time to drive an hour to visit me.

"We felt that the Lord wanted us to get to know you, Carol. He loves you, and has great things in store for you," Bob said.

The Lantzes' excitement about their faith was infectious.

"Why are you so concerned about me?" I asked them. "You hardly even know me."

Charlene smiled shyly and explained, in a soft voice, why she and Bob had taken me by the hand.

"Carol, we believe that we are all called to be servants of the Lord. When God calls for us, we need to obey him. My youngest daughter came home one day and said you were very sick and needed prayer. The Lord gave me a real concern for you. Even though I didn't really know you, I had seen you in town." She laughed and said, "You were always at a half-run, always in a hurry."

I laughed ruefully in agreement.

Charlene went on: "I went to a Bible study and told the others about you, and we prayed for you according to Matt. 18:19. We all realized that someone needed to minister to you and stand fast in faith that you would be healed."

I was amazed. These people hardly even knew who I was, yet they cared enough about me to pray for my health.

"There was silence in the group, and then the Lord began to speak to me. Oh, I didn't want to be the one, I told the Lord." Then the woman standing beside me put her hand on my shoulder, and we both knew I was the one. When I got home, I knew I had to call you and tell you all the Lord had done for me. I kept thinking that I didn't even know you, but the knowledge that I was to call you persisted. 'Call Carol, Call Carol' kept running through my mind. I finally said, 'OK, Lord, I need a word from you.' And immediately, Ps. 81:10 came into mind, which says, 'open thy mouth wide, and I will fill it.' I took my Bible to the desk so I could see that verse, and I dialed your number.''

"Charlene, I am so thankful you did.'' I smiled up at her, impressed at how seriously these two people took their faith.

They talked about the Bible, read some of the Scriptures to me, and assured me that the Bible was as valid today as when it was written.

"Carol, the Lord's Prayer says, 'Thy will be done on earth as it is in heaven.' There's no sickness in heaven,'' said Charlene.

That made sense to me. I was a bit cautious about accepting some of the things I was hearing, but I did believe in heaven, and I did like the Lord's Prayer.

" 'Ask and it shall be given to you, seek and ye shall find, knock and the door shall be opened unto you, it says in Matthew,'' Bob added.

"It isn't God's will for anyone to be sick, Carol. You have to believe that. And he will heal you. Believe that, too,'' Charlene urged.

They read more verses from the Bible to me. One that really stuck in my mind was, "And the prayer of faith shall save the sick, and the Lord shall raise him up,'' from James 5:15. I knew I certainly didn't have strong faith, at least not like Margie and the Lantzes did.

"Have you ever asked Jesus to come into your heart?'' Bob asked.

"I believe in God. I go to church and I pray. Of course I'm a Christian,'' I answered, feeling a bit defensive.

"But, Carol, have you really turned your life over to the Lord? Given him everything—your illness, your life, your marriage?'' he persisted. "Have you trusted him?''

I realized then that I hadn't. I wanted joy and peace and assurance that God was in control. I saw that assurance in Bob and Charlene. Margie had it, too. But something was holding me back. I wanted to be healed, but I just didn't feel the same way about those things as they did.

"The Lord loves you and wants the best for you. He wants to heal you. We have to claim his promises, step out in faith, and believe," Charlene told me.

"Jesus said we should pray for each other. Let's pray for you now," Charlene said before they left. And so we prayed for Jesus to come into my life. He was there all the time, and I believed that he was my Savior and chose me to live eternally. I really wanted to open my heart to him, too, and know him as so many of my Christian friends did, as a friend. Yet something held me back, still, from complete trust and confidence. I knew he was my Savior for eternity, but turning over all my cares and worries here on earth was another thing. I held on to them.

But I finally had time to listen to and think about spiritual matters. I really needed prayers to sustain me, because I grew weaker and weaker. At first the nurses could walk me to the bathroom. I would lock my knees and sort of shuffle along between them.

Then one day in late November, my knees just wouldn't lock anymore and I fell to the floor. After that I was unable to walk independently for a long, long time.

Now the nurses had to bathe me, feed me, dress me, and wash my hair. I was helpless again. Because I had no control over the muscles in my feet, the doctors placed a footboard against the end of the bed. They suggested that Tom buy me some high-top tennis shoes to help prevent footdrop. The shoes were blue and gold with the front cut out because my toes bent backward when we put them on. I had to wear them in bed, and I didn't feel the least bit attractive wearing those shoes!

Physical therapy became an important part of my routine. Every day I was wheeled down to therapy on a stretcher, and I came to know my therapists quite well.

Clyde was in charge of the department. Cliff and Mary Sue were usually my therapists. A volunteer therapist named Ray, who became my special friend, had suffered a stroke and found therapy so helpful that he decided to volunteer and help others recover. Ray really cared about the patients, and I could tell he was truly concerned about me. He was always smiling and would try to get me to laugh and smile. He often said, "Carol, cheer up. You'll get better, too, just like I did."

Despite the valiant efforts of Ray and the others in physical therapy, I kept getting weaker. I thought of how Charlene and Bob said God didn't want me to be sick, and wondered why I wasn't improving.

I had to spend Thanksgiving in a hospital bed. I had planned to be at home making a big turkey dinner for Tom on our first Thanksgiving as a married couple. I didn't feel as if I had very much to be thankful for. Although Tom and my family came to the hospital to visit, turkey on a tray just isn't the same as a big family dinner at home.

By the first of December, I was so weak that I couldn't even turn over. The nurses had to turn me several times a night and block me with pillows. I had never heard of such a thing, but it became a familiar routine. Sleeping a restful, uninterrupted night was impossible.

My legs and arms wouldn't work at all. I was a total quadriplegic, much worse than I had been the first time I was hospitalized five months earlier.

I couldn't lift my arms, move my legs, or do anything but eat, breathe, and talk. Discouragement and despair filled my thoughts.

One day a small woman with a slight German accent came bustling into the room.

"Hello, dear, I'm Katharina," she said. "Bob and Charlene asked me to come and see you."

Katharina and her friend Cynthia became regular visitors. Nearly every day they would stop in and see how I was.

"They don't know me from someone in the street," I thought,

grateful that they would take the time to make my days less lonely. Tom's work prevented him from coming as often as I wanted him to, my sisters worked, and my family all lived more than an hour's drive away. I looked forward to the visits of Katharina and Cynthia.

Arriving with their Bibles, one or both of these unselfish ladies would read to me, pray with me, and just sit with me, keeping me company. Their love for the Lord was obvious in everything they said and did.

"Jesus said that what we do for others is like we are doing it for him," Katharina said one day when I thanked her for her friendship. "Christians help each other."

Despite the prayers and assurances of my friends, I continued to get worse. Double vision set in. Get well cards and Christmas cards were taped all over my room to cheer me up, yet whenever I looked at them and saw several of each, the effect was more depressing than cheering. My attitude wasn't always optimistic. But there was always someone nearby to cheer me up or pray for me when I was down.

Sometimes as Katharina or Cynthia read the Bible to me, I didn't even have the strength or heart to concentrate. Now I realize that God's Word was still ministering to my spirit. They sometimes prayed for God to raise me up from that hospital bed. I wanted to rise up, but I didn't.

Then even more ominous symptoms began to develop. Up to this point, my breathing and swallowing apparently had not been affected. For victims of GBS-like diseases, danger arises when they can't breathe. Sometimes the lung muscles become so paralyzed that they die.

Food started sticking in my throat and my breathing was becoming more and more shallow. Each morning my neurologist would have me take a deep breath and count as far as I could without letting it out. At first I thought it was some sort of game, and I could easily count to 50. It was no game, I soon found, as the count went down to 30, then 15. When you have taken every breath of your life for granted, struggling to breathe is a frightening experience.

Sometimes fear, depression, and anger dragged me down. I resented everyone and everything associated with the hospital and my sickness. I felt guilty for putting Tom through this nightmare. I wondered if he wished he had never married me.

"Divorce me, Tom. Just leave . . . get out of my life," I sobbed sometimes when the depression was the worst. "You don't need a helpless wife. I'm not what you married."

"I'm not leaving you. Stop it," he scolded me. He hated it when I talked like that.

I couldn't help it. It wasn't fair. Tom had married a normal woman, not a helpless baby.

I didn't really mean what I said, and I didn't really want him to leave me, but I felt terrible about dragging him into my ordeal. I decided that if he wanted out, I would let him go without a fight. In fact, I would be the one who had suggested it.

Five days before Christmas, I choked on a cookie that was on my hospital tray. I couldn't get my breath for a minute, which scared my nurse and me. When we told my doctor, he said he was afraid that if I choked on my food, I wouldn't have the strength to cough it back up. I might choke to death. I was shocked; I had never thought of anything like that.

Later that day, my neurologist came into my room and said, "Guess what you're going to get for Christmas."

"What?" I asked.

"A tracheostomy," he answered.

I think he was trying to soften the blow by kidding about it, but I didn't think it was at all funny and I burst into tears.

I cried hysterically for a long time. I knew a tracheostomy meant not being able to talk, a lot of pain, and worst of all, a permanent scar in my throat.

"How much more pain and suffering must I endure, God?"

I cried. *Tom won't be able to look at me,* I thought. *He married a well-kept, size-8 girl—not a skeleton with a pipe in her throat.*

A compassionate nun who visited hospital patients learned that I needed a trach and came to see me. I was crying too hard to call Tom, so she phoned him for me. I was so grateful to her for explaining to Tom what a trach was. I didn't want him to drive all the way to Toledo and find me with a trach, unable to talk and explain what had happened.

The doctors performed the tracheostomy surgery that day around 6 p.m. I didn't understand exactly what a trach did, so one of the doctors explained that they would make an incision in my throat and insert a tube down into my lungs. This tube was sutured into place and stuck out of a hole in the hollow of my throat. Instead of breathing through my nose or mouth, I would breathe through this tube.

I didn't care how much the trach would help me, I was upset and angry as they wheeled me off to surgery. When I awoke, I was in intensive care and couldn't utter a sound. My throat hurt terribly and it was extremely painful each time I swallowed.

"This is the worst pain I have ever experienced," I thought.

At times I thought it was more pain than I could cope with. I wanted to know why God had let this happen to me.

"Why, God? Why me? Why now? I'm only 28, not 98!"

The nurses gave me pain shots, but still the pain was often unbearable. IVs were hooked up to my body, and all the tubes and wires attached to me made me feel like I was just part of a machine.

My night nurse, Carol, was a pretty, cheerful woman who decided I needed some method to ring for a nurse. Since I was too paralyzed to ring a buzzer and couldn't yell, she crocheted a headband for me and put a bell on it. Then she attached her creation to the IV pole in such a way that when I tossed my head slightly, the bell would ring. This worked fine, except that occasionally the headband slipped off, and then I would be helpless again.

The nurses used a chart of letters to communicate with me, because I couldn't even write. By pointing to the letters and watching my eyes blink, they would see which letter I was indicating. In this time-consuming, sometimes frustrating manner, we would spell out words such as "pain shot," "bedpan," or whatever else I needed. The chart was a far cry from being able to stand in front of my classes and lecture, talking a mile a minute, but it was better than nothing.

The next day the nurses tried to get me to eat some gelatin. Each time I swallowed, my throat felt as if it would tear open. It wasn't worth the pain, so I ate nothing that day.

I tried to accept what was happening to me, but I just couldn't. When I cried, tears ran down my face and filled my ears, and there was no way I could wipe them away.

I was in intensive care for several days after my surgery. I preferred that unit, not only because I was so sick, but because there was always a lot of hubbub and activity, and it helped me take my mind off myself. The nurses were nice and extremely capable, and I felt secure.

Because of the trach, I had to be suctioned quite often. The noises—gushing, gurgling sounds—were unappetizing, and it was undoubtedly nauseating to watch as the nurses cleaned out the secretions from my throat opening.

Several days later, I was returned to a regular room. Since I had so many monitors hooked up to me, the nurses shoved the other bed against the wall rather than give me a roommate. The monitor used to measure my breathing was nicknamed "Harvey." If my breathing became too shallow, Harvey would cause a buzzer to ring. For some reason, Harvey never did cooperate. I was breathing easily with the trach, but Harvey would sound off frequently, day and night, making it impossible for me or those nearby to sleep.

After several days of putting up with Harvey's irritating ring, I was relieved when the doctors finally decided that the trach was sufficient. I was glad to be rid of the contrary Harvey. I felt more comfortable with the tracheostomy and was beginning to adjust to the pain.

It was a good thing I had decided to accept the trach. It was my partner for quite a while.

5

TOM AND I SPENT OUR FIRST CHRISTMAS as a couple apart. I insisted, by mouthing words, that he spend the holiday with his family. I couldn't talk, eat, or open gifts, and I really didn't want him to have to sit there with me by himself. When I had first been admitted to the hospital, we had both hoped I would be home by Christmas. But that didn't happen.

So I spent Christmas in a hospital bed. Thoughts of Christmases past filled my mind, and hopes for better Christmases also entered. I hoped I would only have to spend one Christmas in the hospital.

I had plenty of time to think as I lay in that bed. There was time to reflect on the true meaning of Christmas. In the past I had been too busy buying gifts, going to parties, and visiting people to think much about the true meaning of Christmas. Now I thought about the meaning of Jesus' birth and life and death. I did pray quite a bit that day, and as usual I asked him to heal my body as soon as possible.

I often felt guilty for my depression and irritability. I wish I could say that I placidly accepted all my trials and confidently assumed everything was working for the best, but I didn't.

Although I loved God, I still felt he was being terribly unfair to me.

Determined to recover, I continued physical therapy. My muscles had to be exercised regularly so they wouldn't stiffen. Many of my visitors learned to do "range of motion" exercises, moving my arms and legs in circles.

I was so thankful for the visitors who took the time to come and see me. My teacher friends as well as my principal, Dave Rex, and his wife Sharon, came and kept me up-to-date with news of the school and students. Even the high school superintendent, Richard Harris, and his wife Dee, came to visit. Tom's mom and dad, my dad, and other friends all came when they could. My sisters and Tom's sisters helped me with my needs.

"What would I do without these people showing their concern?" I often thought.

I felt sorry for the patients who didn't have many visitors. Lying alone, day after day, in a hospital bed can be terribly lonely.

Much of the time I was too sick to be very sociable. Besides, it's hard to be witty and bright with a tube in your throat.

I couldn't see well enough to read, and when a Christian family from Archbold gave me a tape recorder, I used it often to play scripture and sermon tapes from my sister Margie and from Charlene and Bob. Gil and Rose Lewis, friends of Charlene and Bob, came often and shared Scripture. They talked enthusiastically about their faith. Another Christian couple, Gert and Bud Hitt, also began coming to see me regularly, and they brought New Testament tapes. Many times I was in so much pain that I couldn't concentrate on the tapes, but I played them anyway. Sometimes I went to sleep by their sound.

Often when I had visitors, I felt as though I were in a daze. I wanted to smile and make them feel good about coming to see me, but I just wasn't up to it.

In addition to the double vision, there was still the pain of swallowing. Even after I had become accustomed to the tube, there was still pain. *Had I been totally paralyzed with a spinal injury, at least I wouldn't have had this much pain,* I once thought bitterly. I immediately regretted my thought, because I was glad I still had feeling in my body.

As soon as I was able to swallow, I was put on a diet of strained cream soups. I drank some milk, but milk and ice cream caused more secretions, and the nurses would have to suction the phlegm several times during the meal. It was frightening, unappetizing, and a lot of bother.

"Whoever thinks about trying to breathe, being suctioned, and swallowing at the same time?" I thought to myself during an especially messy meal. "*I* never did when I was gulping down pizzas back home."

Some of the nurses were especially helpful and made me feel like I was more than just a patient. Marilyn, a student nurse, took me on as a special project. Her dorm was nearby, and she often stopped by just to chat and check up on me. I wondered if people realize how much little gestures like that mean to those who are sick or lonely.

My nurse, Linda, and I became close friends during my stay. I felt a spiritual tie to Linda, and was so glad whenever I was her patient. She seemed to understand me better than most people could, which made my life less frustrating. I also knew she was praying for me, and cared about me as a person, not just a patient.

I was certain that Linda's sensitivity and love stemmed from her love for the Lord. What other explanation could there be for her behavior, and the similar concern shown by Katharina, Cynthia, Bob, Charlene, Rose, Gil, and other Christians who weren't my family or previous friends?

I really looked forward to the cheerful, encouraging visits of these Christian friends, and their constant assurances that God was doing great things in my life. I considered myself to be a Christian, yet I sensed a great difference between my faith and theirs.

I wanted to believe as they did, but something held me back. Faithfully and lovingly, my Christian friends prayed for me, and during that long, cold winter I came to understand who Jesus really is. I saw his love in action, through the love shown to me. I learned about his life and promises through scripture tapes and listening as someone read the Bible to me. And I felt that I was getting to know a new God, a God who was not only the Savior who loved us enough to become human and die that we might have eternal life, but a God who truly is Lord of all. I finally understood that he would be the Lord of my life here on earth if I would just let him.

I knew that I wanted to turn over my whole life to the Lord, not just to heal me on earth, but to trust him with my life now and forever. I wanted the same assurance and peace that I saw in so many of my Christian friends.

So as I lay paralyzed in a hospital bed, helpless and alone, I prayed for the Holy Spirit to help me grow spiritually and be a real, living presence in me day to day. There were no inner fireworks or tears, and I didn't get up and shout "Praise the Lord" (with my trach, I couldn't have done that anyway!), but there was a deep conviction that at last I was doing the right thing.

I felt a warmth and joy in my heart that seemed out of place after all the anguish and despair of the past months. Nobody wants to be sick, but perhaps that was the only way I would listen long enough to know who the Lord is. Before, I lived for myself. I went to church on Sundays, but I had never really known Jesus personally. I had always been much too busy and in charge of things to seriously think much about him. I hated being so sick, of course, but now I slowly began to realize that the Lord can work in every circumstance of life, no matter how terrible, if we just let him. Even in this tragedy, there was good. I was finally still long enough to realize that he is Lord.

I wish I could say that life was uphill after that. It wasn't. My faith grew, sometimes in leaps and bounds, especially when I was doing well physically, and sometimes in little turtle-steps.

Sometimes, after a bad day or lonely, pain-filled night, it shrank a little. Sometimes I was irritable, jealous, confused, and upset. But through it all, Jesus was there. I knew his love was constant, even when mine wasn't. He was working in my life.

Charlene, Bob, Linda, and the rest of my friends and family wouldn't let me get discouraged. They continued coming to pray with me, read the Scriptures, and just talk about the Lord. When I couldn't seem to pray for myself, they prayed for me. Their faith bolstered me when mine sagged.

Tom wasn't as excited about my new commitment as I was. He was happy that I felt so much peace inside, but he was a bit skeptical of it all, especially the fact that I fully expected the Lord to heal me.

"Carol, I don't know. That sounds too good to be true," he said hesitantly. I had gotten the message across to him through mouthing, spelling, and just plain happiness. He wanted me to get well, too, but he had seen what dashed hopes had done to me before. Tom loved God too, and belonged to the church, but he didn't know what to make of all this talk about healing, claiming Bible promises, and having a personal relationship with Jesus.

I had discovered an amazing thing. We could go to church regularly, listen to good sermons, and associate with other Christians, but unless we were open to letting Jesus take over our lives as Lord and Savior, we could go through life without ever knowing Christ as a real, living presence. We might think that being a Christian is just a matter of following certain rules or standards, without knowing why. At least that had been my experience. I wondered how many people I had sat beside in church pews who didn't actually know the Lord.

I don't think the Lord favors Christians of one denomination over another. I honestly believe God doesn't care if we are Catholic, Lutheran, Mennonite, or Assembly of God, as long as we love and honor him, believe in Jesus as Savior, and follow the Bible. I know that many Christians of different denominations were praying for me.

I was praying for healing and claiming Bible verses about healing. "I will take sickness away from the midst of thee" (Exod. 23:25). Psalm 103 says, "Bless the Lord, O my soul, and forget not all his benefits: Who forgiveth all thine iniquities; who healeth all thy diseases" (vv. 2-3). "Jesus went about all Galilee, teaching in their synagogues, and preaching the gospel of the kingdom, and healing all manner of sickness and all manner of disease among the people" (Matt. 4:23) is a verse that gave me much hope.

Still, I couldn't move my arms and legs. Sometimes I thought, "Lord, why don't you give me an instant miracle?" But I knew deep down that it isn't for us to tell the Lord what to do. Over and over again I was trying to boss God around.

I had times of improvement and times of setback. Sometimes I felt as though I was on display, like the times the doctors changed my trach tube. Once a month the tube had to be replaced to prevent infection. As they pulled out the old and put in the new, six or eight resident doctors gathered around my bedside, watching the procedure so they could learn how to do it.

My chest had to be X-rayed quite often to make sure I wasn't developing pneumonia or complications. I didn't like having so many X-rays, but there didn't seem to be any way around them.

Several people were needed to do everything for me. They would lift me up, move me from bed to stretcher and back again. I felt like a nonstop bother.

Then the hot flashes started. I became known as "the girl with the washcloths" because the nurses put cold washcloths on my hands when my body felt like it was burning up. My hands felt like they were on fire, and they would actually cook the cloths dry. The hot flashes came on suddenly, without warning, and the nurses would quickly try to sponge me off so I would cool down. This went on for about five months. Being known as "the girl with the washcloths" was kind of funny, but the terrible pain wasn't.

I could no longer effectively communicate with those around me, yet I was totally dependent on them for all my needs. Tom became quite good at reading my lips and watching my eyes for signals. We developed our own private language. Because Tom knew me so well, and tried so hard, he could usually understand what I needed or wanted better than the doctors or nurses could.

My family tried not to let on how worried they were about me, but it showed in their faces. I am especially close to my sisters, and Margie wrote from the Virgin Islands and asked that we keep her informed about my condition.

My dad came to visit me in the hospital when he could, though his farm was more than 100 miles away. I could tell that it bothered him terribly to see me so sick, especially after losing my mom. In February of 1978 he wrote Margie the following letter:

> *I called the hospital and got to talk to Carol. They put a plug in that oxygen outfit so she could talk to me. She talked like always, except a little slow, as it seemed to use up all her strength. I let Mike talk to her also. When she would get tired, she would stop a little but then go on again.*

Once in awhile, my nurse would put a cap on the trach and I could talk for a few minutes. It wore me out, but was worth it to be able to talk again for a bit.

I loved hearing my dad's voice. It brought back memories of growing up on the farm, playing outside with my sisters and brothers, and happier days.

"I'll be able to visit Dad at the farm again," I promised myself.

Margie also received a letter from Charlene about the same time, describing my condition—both physical and spiritual:

> *Dear Sister in the Lord: We just came home after having a blessed time with Carol, and see Him doing a mighty*

work in her life and body. We really love your sister. You can be so very proud of her. She is so special to us. We praise God He laid her on our hearts, even though we didn't know her. We just say thank you Jesus for leading us to Carol. We have seen a big change in Carol, a beautiful change taking place. She is praising the Lord and claiming healing. . . . There are two ladies, Katharina and Cynthia, who go every day and read the Word of God to her and pray with her. The Lord laid it on my heart to call Carol when she was home yet, to tell her what the Lord had done in my life and the many healings that have taken place. I was supposed to be a wheelchair patient. PTL, I am healed. We didn't know Carol and she didn't know us. Isn't it just like Jesus to bring people together?

We try to go down and see Carol every Friday evening. We just praise the Lord for this opportunity to minister to Carol. We're just claiming Carol to rise up and walk in the name of Jesus. And she will. There are many people who are fasting and praying and God knows and hears the prayers of his saints. My husband and I are both in our late forties. We feel like spiritual parents to Carol, and want the very best for her. Keep on praying. God is answering our prayers and we praise Him for it.

My condition remained the same through February and into March. I was still quadriplegic and experienced double vision off and on. Many times daily, I would choke and the secretions would build up in my throat. Then the nurses had to suction me.

When Charlene and Bob came to visit, they brought a copy of the Archbold *Buckeye.* Charlene would hold the paper for me as I caught up on hometown news. Then they would pray with me and build me up spiritually. I looked forward to their visits and the encouragement they gave me.

In early March, my condition improved enough that I was able to begin eating pureed baby foods.

"Yuk," was my reaction the first time I saw my meal of pureed meats and vegetables.

"Let's try some real food, Carol," said Linda as she brought the mushy food to my bedside. The fruits and vegetables weren't bad, but the meat was awful.

I'd rather have a pureed pizza, I thought.

A few days after the baby food meal, I was able to eat soft foods, which was a real accomplishment. I hadn't eaten anything as solid as mashed potatoes in months.

"I think we can keep the cap on for longer periods of time," my doctor decided one day. We had been capping the trach occasionally so I could talk to visitors or on the phone, but never for very long. I enjoyed being able to talk, and became used to breathing through my nose and mouth again.

One night toward the end of March, my doctor decided to cap my trach all night to see how I would sleep without it. Fear gripped me. As much as I wanted to breathe on my own, and be rid of the pipe in my throat, I had come to depend on the trach as my safeguard. Instead of putting my trust in the Lord to watch over me as I slept, I found I was putting my trust in the trach.

We decided to try it, however, and I slept pretty well. My doctor decided I was strong enough to breathe alone.

"Today the trach comes out," he announced the next day.

I was still afraid, despite my doctor's assurances.

What if I choke? What if I can't breathe? I wondered.

The head doctor of respiratory therapy pulled the tube out of my throat, and within several hours the hole closed up. I could tell I would have a big scar, but there was nothing to be done about it. The tube was out, and I could talk again.

Tom was delighted that we could finally carry on a decent conversation.

"Now you'll probably never stop talking," he teased.

About this time, Margie received a letter from my sister Judy, who lived in Columbus and came to visit when she could:

Last Saturday I drove up to see Carol with Darlene and Theresa. Carol is as well as can be expected. Very slow progress and reasonably good spirits, considering the situation and the fact that she's been cooped up for so long. We spent Saturday afternoon with her. We saw Carol's Tom last weekend, also. He is working 12-hour shifts and only gets to visit Carol on weekends, which is hard on both of them. Carol and Tom are both thin as rails. Tom did seem to be in better spirits than last time we saw him, but he's still very quiet and seems to be holding it all inside. Carol's doctor told me he's never had a case of GBS as bad as hers. Carol is certainly not giving up, though, but as many things go, it doesn't seem fair.

My progress seemed terribly slow. I was determined to walk again, and I continued physical therapy. I still couldn't move any muscles on my own, so my P.T. consisted mainly of having therapists move my limbs around for me.

One Saturday, the nurse who bathed me forgot to tie my hospital gown. The therapist moved me from a stretcher to a tilt table and raised it to a standing position to help my body grow accustomed to a position other than horizontal. A few minutes later, my gown slid off one shoulder, and there wasn't a thing I could do about it.

I couldn't reach down and pull it up, and several rather personal parts of my anatomy were exposed for the whole room to see.

I looked around in dismay for one of the woman therapists. None was to be seen. None of the female patients was in any condition to come over and help me, either.

Finally realizing that I had no choice, I yelled over to Cliff. "Please come and help me," I called as quietly as I could.

Cliff turned bright red, chuckled at my predicament, and hurried over to fix my gown. I think he was as embarrassed as I was!

We both soon got over our embarrassment. When you're incapacitated, you learn not to be as modest as you normally are, or you would be in a perpetual state of shame. I never did get used to some things, though, such as male nurses, even though they were competent and caring.

The therapists were good with me. My volunteer therapist friend, Ray, was especially concerned about me.

One day he gave me a cross that said, "He lives," and he said with a smile, "Someday, Carol, I want you to hand this cross back to me."

I thought about my paralyzed arms and hands, and I realized how much faith he had that I would walk and use my hands again.

I smiled at him, fighting back tears. That cross and his faith in Jesus meant a lot to me. Then and there I decided I would indeed hand it back to him someday.

Cliff and I became good friends also. When I felt overwhelmed and bewildered by my situation, he would console me and dry the tears I couldn't wipe away.

"Now, Carol, don't you cry. You'll be OK," he would say gently. "Jesus will never leave you or forsake you." He talked to me like my own father would, and once or twice he even kissed me on the forehead after an especially long, soul-searching talk. Sometimes Cliff and his wife Flora would stop in my room to see how I was doing, and I grew to love them.

I continued to pray and claim Bible verses about healing. I was still upset about my paralysis, but with my new commitment to the Lord came a peace I hadn't known before. "Somehow it will all make sense, if I can just hang in there," I told myself.

My new commitment was soon tested. I had been very optimistic that I would improve and recover completely, but my doctors didn't agree.

In April, my condition was stable. I couldn't move, but I could eat and breathe easily. My neurologist asked Tom to come to the hospital for a talk.

"Tom and Carol, I want to discuss your future. I think you should know what we feel is ahead for you," he said. "Carol, your nerve damage is probably permanent. You have been paralyzed for so long that it's highly unlikely that your muscles will ever function properly again."

"Are you saying that I'll never walk again? That I'll always be a quadriplegic?" I cried.

Tom was stunned. Neither of us had considered the possibility that my condition would be permanent. We couldn't think about that. It was too terrible.

"In my opinion, if you ever walk again, or regain use of your muscles, it will be in the distant future. We can discuss a long-term recovery plan, but you may never recover. Or you may have relapse after relapse. You have to face the fact that it's highly unlikely that you will ever be normal. I suggest that you just accept your quadriplegia, and plan your life with that as part of it," he said as gently as possible.

I could tell it was hard on the doctor to give us such negative news, but for Tom and I it was devastating.

He went on to say that he was afraid I would work and work to regain some strength and get my hopes up, only to suffer recurrences of the disease. Even if the disease ever did burn itself out, he was afraid the damage to my nervous system would be irreversible.

I was angry. I knew I had been given the best care available for GBS and similar conditions at that time, and I trusted my doctor, but I couldn't accept this. I felt he was telling me to give up and accept my paralysis.

I burst into tears. Tom was strong and listened calmly to what the doctor said. "I'm sorry, I really am," the doctor said as he left my room.

I sobbed, "Tom, I just cannot accept this. I just can't. I really believe that with God all things are possible."

We agreed to continue to pray that I would recover and that we would be able to have a normal, happy marriage together.

"God can change any diagnosis," I said, remembering the

promises my friends had shared with me, and the Scriptures I had read.

That God could heal me, I knew. Yet I also knew of wonderful, committed Christians who weren't healed. Why not? Why were some healed and others not? The question haunted me.

6

"Do you want to go to a healing service, Carol?" Charlene asked in May. I could tell she was excited. "Charles and Frances Hunter will be here at the auditorium, and I think we should go."

I was willing to work hard at getting well, but I knew God could heal me in an instant, without all that work. Maybe I needed to demonstrate my faith. I decided to go.

Charlene and Bob and several friends signed me out of the hospital, with special permission, for a few hours. I went through the prayer line in a wheelchair, helpless, and the Hunters laid their hands on me and prayed for my healing.

I closed my eyes tight and prayed hard. I hoped I would leap out of that wheelchair, whole again. Although I didn't, I still held onto my hope. We went back to the hospital after the service, and I was still paralyzed.

I really did think that God would heal me instantly, but since he didn't, I thought, *Well, when I wake up in the morning, I'll be healed.*

I felt you had to have faith to believe that God can grant miracles in order to receive a miracle, and I was trying to stand on my faith. When I woke up in the morning, I was still paralyzed and quite confused. Was my faith too weak? What about all my friends who had been praying so faithfully for me? It was a mystery to me, but Bob and Charlene said to keep believing and to trust God.

About this time I met a student nurse who was in her late thirties. She came into my room to chat, and suddenly asked me, "What disease do you have, Carol?" When I told her, she said, "I had GBS 20 years ago in Germany."

"You did? You seem OK," I told her, excited to meet someone who had suffered GBS and had recovered.

She told me how much trouble she had had with the disease, and how she struggled to gain her strength again. She hadn't been as bad as I was, but it still gave me a real lift to see that she was doing so well.

"The only thing I really can't do is run," she said.

"I feel like God sent you here to give me hope," I told her.

With a smile, she left. She had so much energy that I was impressed and envious.

I was scheduled to be dismissed from the hospital on June 5, nearly a year after Tom and I had been married. Still unable to walk, sit up alone, or use my arms, I could only talk, breathe, and swallow. The doctor suggested that I go home because he couldn't do any more for me in the hospital. He advised me to get a wheelchair, bedpan, hospital bed, and portable hydraulic lift.

I resisted this. I wouldn't accept permanent or long-term paralysis. Always feisty, I found myself insisting that he help me find a place to go where I could get physical therapy.

"Carol, just go home," he suggested gently.

"No. Physical therapy helped me once. I'm sure it will work. Send me someplace where I can have lots of therapy," I demanded, taking matters into my own hands.

For many people who have been sick, rehabilitation centers are the perfect places to recuperate. For me, a center was the wrong place to be. I realized later that I should have listened to my doctor. He gave in to my insistence, and made arrangements to have me transferred to a rehabilitation center.

The day before I left the hospital, the nurses and staff threw a going-away party for me. We had cake and ice cream, and they gave me a gift to remember them by—as if I could ever forget my 6½-month stay, and all my experiences and the people I had grown close to! I had good care there, by my doctors, nurses, and the staff, and I knew I would miss them.

As Tom and his parents gathered my clothes, cards, and plants, I said good-bye to my doctors and nurses. As they wheeled me down to the car, I planned my return—on foot. Although I had hoped to walk out of the hospital, I felt certain that I would walk back in someday, just to say hello.

We drove directly to the rehabilitation center, arriving near lunchtime. When we arrived, one of the attendants came up to the car.

He helped me into a wheelchair, and then proceeded to tie me in.

"Hey! What are you doing?" I asked.

"We have to tie you in so you don't fall out," he replied.

It was bad enough that I couldn't get out of that chair, but I certainly didn't want to be tied in.

Tom explained that I had been in a chair for awhile and had never fallen out, and finally the attendant agreed not to tie me.

People were in wheelchairs everywhere, and many were moaning and groaning. A lot of people didn't seem to be in their right minds. I lost my appetite and couldn't eat much.

I was so exhausted that I went to bed at 6 p.m. The next morning, an aide dressed me. I had worn nothing but hospital gowns for the past six months, except on special occasions, so I was glad that the center's policy was to dress us every day. It was a good psychological lift.

My roommate, Joyce, was 37 and semiparalyzed from an aneurism. Her head was shaved and she wore a wig that she called her "rug." Her sense of humor was delightful, and she was a joy to be near.

"Your name suits you," I told her soon after we met.

I got to know some of the other patients, too. Greg was 26 and a multiple sclerosis victim. His disease was affecting both his eyesight and his muscles. Suzie, 22, had been in a terrible car accident and couldn't walk. There were so many tragic cases. In both of the hospitals where I had stayed I had been one of the worst cases. Now I was surrounded by others just as bad.

My days began with breakfast, occupational therapy, and then physical therapy. After lunch, O.T. and P.T. were repeated. I usually went to bed around 8 or 9 p.m., tired from sitting in my wheelchair all day.

Pat, Sandy, and Jean, my occupational therapists, came to be my closest friends at the rehab center. They made a mouthstick for me and urged me to use it on the keys of a typewriter. I didn't want to. I thought it was degrading, and besides, my idea of therapy wasn't learning how to adjust to my paralysis, but to *beat* it.

"Come on, Carol, just type a little," urged Pat, putting the stick between my teeth. I didn't really want to, but I did want to send a note to Tom, so I typed a brief letter.

This is just until I get my fingers back, I decided as I painstakingly picked out each letter.

Later I typed out a diary with the mouthstick, did some painting, and realized that it was a handy little gadget. But I still saw it as only a temporary tool.

My bright idea of doing a lot of therapy and having a quick recovery wasn't working. I wasn't improving at all. I was lonely, and because the center was even farther from home than the hospital, Tom could not come as often.

Our first wedding anniversary was two weeks after I entered the rehab center. With my doctor's approval, Tom and I planned for me to come home. I was thrilled to be able to spend some time with Tom again. I was still so helpless that when Bob and

Charlene suggested we spend the weekend in their home, we accepted, grateful for their help.

It wasn't the kind of first anniversary we had anticipated, but we had a pleasant weekend in spite of my paralysis.

Tom drove me back to the rehab center on Sunday night. Luckily, our van had reclining seats, so the ride was fairly comfortable.

I began living for the weekends, when I could leave and go home with Tom. I worked hard in therapy all week, and weekends were my time to relax. I was so much work for Tom and my family and friends, though, that sometimes I felt guilty about leaving the center, where they were paid to care for all my needs.

July 3 was my 29th birthday. When the aide asked what I wanted (patients are allowed to order anything on their birthdays), I responded with enthusiasm, "Pizza!" Tom was coming, and I wanted to share it with him.

I attacked the pizza with enthusiasm, but wasn't able to swallow very well.

Oh, no. Not again, I thought, knowing all too well what swallowing problems indicated. Tom had to eat most of the pizza.

As he wheeled me down the hall to the door, the light reflecting from the chrome machines and the colorful designs on the walls hurt my eyes. I had noticed double vision on and off the past few days, but again, I tried to deny it.

Tom lifted me into the van and we drove to our house. My dad and my sisters and brothers came the next day to celebrate my birthday and the Fourth of July. We invited Charlene and Bob, too, and we all had a good time. I couldn't get any food down, but I tried not to let on. I didn't want anything to spoil the day.

Charlene and Bob gave me a latch-hook rug kit reading "The Lord Is My Shepherd." I always enjoyed handwork, and used to knit for half an hour every night on an afghan or other project.

"We want you to hook this rug, Carol," Charlene smiled.

Looking down at my motionless hands and fingers, I thought, *These two have so much faith. I can't let them down!*

Back at the rehab center again, the nurses switched me to a liquid diet after I choked for an hour and a half on a french fry. Choking was a terrifying experience. Weird sounds came out of me, I couldn't relax, and phlegm and mucous kept building up until I had to spit it out. The liquid diet was monotonous, but it was better than choking. My throat was getting too weak to swallow anything solid, and my lungs were too weak to cough things up.

My voice grew weaker and weaker, until it was a tremendous effort to talk at all. People around me probably thought I was unfriendly, but I just had no strength to chat. Even smiling was an effort.

I was like a limp dishrag, and had no control of my arms, legs, or neck. My head would fall back whenever someone put me in a wheelchair.

"Lord, help me bear this," I prayed. "And please help Tom."

I felt that I had made a mistake by coming there. I wasn't getting any better and I was lonely and wanted to go home. But I didn't want to be a burden to Tom. I was even more work now than I had been a month before. I cried, I hoped, and I prayed for a miracle.

The visitors who drove several hours to see me made my days easier. Tom, our families, my friends, my fellow teachers, and some of the nurses and therapists from the hospital were my most regular visitors. I was really surprised that my former nurse Linda and therapists Cliff and Ray would take the time after their own hospital work to drive all that way to visit.

One summer Saturday I was pleasantly surprised by a visit from two home economics teachers from Archbold and 15 of my former students. They presented me with a patchwork quilt the girls had embroidered and quilted. I was touched that they would work so hard on a gift for me, but also embarrassed that they should see me so helpless. I wondered what they were thinking. I tried to put everyone at ease by smiling a lot, but deep inside I wanted to burst into tears.

"God, please heal me. I want to be better and show all these people how much their concern means to me," I prayed. I was determined to repay as many kindnesses as I could. I was a mixture of trust and impatience, of faith and fear. St. Paul's observation that "what I would do, that I do not; but what I hate, that do I" (Rom. 7:15) often described my attitude.

Most of the people who worked at the rehab center genuinely cared about the patients. For example, Jane was a nurse who was special to me, and she would take me outside for fresh air during her breaks. However, there were some who were insensitive, and these made living there less bearable.

Because I could barely talk, some people apparently thought I couldn't hear or think, either. To be treated as though I were mentally incapacitated and talked about as if I wasn't there was upsetting.

I'm afraid, though, that I wasn't always a very good example of Christian perseverance. God was working in my life, but I kept letting my situation get to me. Then depression would threaten to overwhelm me.

I didn't want to accept quadriplegia. I just could not believe this was God's will for my life. Why would God drag Tom into such an ordeal? Why newlyweds? No, I really did believe he wanted me to be healthy again. Maybe some people could accept paralysis. I couldn't.

There would be times I would be optimistic and cheerful, and times I would let the joy of my salvation carry me through the discouragement. But there were many other days that were sad and dark. I was a study of conflicting emotions. Depression is terrible, and it can defeat you. Thank the Lord, my faithful friends Charlene, Bob, Rose, Gil, Katharina, and Cynthia, and my family and others vigilantly kept praying for me and standing on God's word to heal me.

Often I was irritable and impatient. Sometimes jealousy welled up inside me, and try as I would to control it, it would make me think that anyone who could move had it better than I did. I would try to fight down these bitter feelings, but they rose to the surface anyway. It's easy to smile and be pleasant and agreeable when life is going your way, I realized. Now I had to deal with some less lovely parts of myself.

I wanted my friends and sisters to realize how much little things should mean to them and not take their health for granted. I figured that if I had to go through this, at least I could pass on what I was learning.

One night a friend was visiting me. She was tired and a bit depressed.

"What could you be depressed about? It's a beautiful day and you can walk and eat by yourself and go home to your family. I'm stuck here for who knows how long," I said. She looked hurt.

One night one of my friends was direct and honest with me. "Carol, you are hard to take care of sometimes, did you know that?"

I was hurt and surprised. I thought she was my friend.

"Why?" I asked her.

"Partly because of your age. You're so young, and have a new husband, and I guess it's easy to think, *What if that were me?* But the main thing is that you are always telling people that things in their lives can't be so bad. You seem to think other people's problems just don't exist. Sometimes, maybe they just want you to listen instead of telling them to count their blessings. Other people have problems, too, you know," she said.

Her words opened my eyes, and I began to see what she meant. I had been heaping guilt on my family and friends. We can't judge other people, because we don't know what they have gone through. Everyone has problems, no matter how physically sick or healthy he or she may be.

Sometimes I would scold myself, and despair of ever growing to be the kind of Christian I should be. Then I would remember Rom. 3:23, "all have sinned, and come short of the glory of

God," and remind myself that I wasn't the first and won't be the last person to fail.

I read my Bible, using my mouthstick to turn the pages. We had regular Friday night worship and prayer services, with Bob and Charlene or Rose and Gil giving me a special message each time.

A chiropractor who had helped me swallow more easily also came to visit me at the rehabilitation center. Dr. Mull was a kind and concerned man who even opened his office once for me on a holiday when my swallowing was difficult. He didn't charge us for his services, and his treatments helped relax my throat muscles.

It always touched me that so many went out of their way to help Tom and me. The schools in Archbold and Ridgeville, my church in Archbold, and community members of both towns worked together to put on a benefit dinner for us. They raised $11,000 for help with our medical bills.

"Tom, the Lord provides," I said. "We've been so worried about the bills, and this will help." At first we had both hesitated to accept money from others, but then I realized the Bible tells us to help those in need, and we were certainly in need. Through these loving, unselfish people the Lord gave us money to pay off some bills. We gratefully accepted this gift of love from our friends and neighbors.

My little mouthstick and my typewriter came in handy when I decided to keep a short diary of what was going on in my life. I recorded events and visitors, and it seemed to help me keep a perspective on what was happening:

August 3, 1978

I'm in occupational therapy—typing with a mouthstick. I have been here since June 5. I am having much difficulty swallowing.

Presently I can only drink liquids. I weigh about 102 lbs. I have lost 10 to 12 lbs. since June. I am seeking to know more about God and all of the great and good promises he has for each of us. Life seems almost unbearable at times.

My husband is being very strong through this tremendous struggle confronting us. I see him every weekend. Last weekend I stayed at Shirley & Don's.

August 4

I ate a poached egg & an eggnog for breakfast—½ of a banana also. I'm going to Wauseon for the weekend again. Bob, Charlene, & Dawn Lantz came up to get me 'cause Tom works nights at La Choy.

August 10

Friday night Cliff and Flora came to see me.

Last Sunday, 8/6, was Tom's birthday—he turned 30.

I'm able to eat poached or soft-cooked eggs, cream of wheat, pureed foods. After last Mon. I noticed improvement in my swallowing; of course, there is still a lot of need for improvement.

Tom is on vacation this week and also will be on vacation the week of the 21st. Tom, Charlene, Bob, & Dawn, & Carol H. all came to see me last nite. I might go home for the weekend. Tom plays softball each Sun.

There are several people here that I can confide in—two occupational therapists—Pat & Jeanne. They are great friends.

August 17

Things have been going better. I stayed here last weekend. Tom & I went out Sat. nite. He hit some balls at the driving range nearby. Then he got some ice cream. Dad & Uncle Junior came Sat. nite.

As of last Sat. I am on a soft diet—ground meat, potatoes, etc. I gained a pound. This Sat. I am going home for a week vacation. Therese will help out that week.

Bob, Charlene, & Mrs. Weldy all came last nite. They are all very dear to me.

I am making small amounts of progress physically. No double vision.

August 30

Well, I'm back here again—got back yesterday. I had a 9-day vacation at home. Tom & Therese took care of me.

Had lots of company while home . . . including Marge, Rob, Faith, Dar, Dean, Pat, Rich, etc. Of course, Bob, Charlene, Dawn, & Sandy came lots.

Things went pretty well while I was home. I was able to eat such foods as tomatoes, green beans, potatoes, toast, some meat, etc.

Sunday nite, however, I choked on some hamburger and coughed for more than two hours—it was horrible. That same nite (around 3 a.m.) I got sick.

I started drinking carrot & celery juice as of last Sat. Uncle Junior loaned us a juicer. I'm trying to drink several glasses daily. I'm also taking food supplements—they taste absolutely HORRIBLE!!!

I wish I could be home with my husband every day—doing all the things a wife likes to do for her husband. I love Tom sooo.

August 31

Eyes and throat seem to be acting up again. Some double vision when looking at things while lying down. Can swallow OK but it is harder to swallow than it was several days ago. Bob

& Charlene came last nite—don't know what I'd do without them!!! Plan to go home Sat.—Mon. Mon. is Labor Day. There was an article in the Buckeye this week . . . there is going to be a benefit dinner in Archbold to raise $ for Tom & me.

Life is so hard to understand—I guess I don't really understand it at all.

Morris Cerello is going to be in Columbus in Oct. I definitely want to go!!!

7

B Y MID-SEPTEMBER, I WAS SO WEAK again that I had difficulty holding my head up. Tom came to pick me up for a weekend visit.

This has to be so depressing for Tom, to see his wife like this again, I thought.

If Tom was upset, he didn't show it. He loaded me into the van and we drove home.

Bob and Charlene came to visit, and they noticed my discouragement.

"Carol, don't you give up," Charlene said. "The Lord will heal you. Remember Psalm 103, 'Bless the Lord, O my soul, and forget not all his benefits: Who forgiveth all thine iniquities; who healeth all thy diseases.' "

They all laid hands on me and prayed for my body, spirit, and emotions. Although I was still physically weak, my spirits were lifted.

We always had time to talk about the Lord when Bob and Charlene came. They shared many Scripture verses with me. Most of them I had read on my own, but talking about them with other Christians helped me to realize how true they were.

One of my favorites, a verse that boosted me when my faith wasn't enough, was Eph. 2:8: "For by grace are ye saved through faith; and that is not of yourselves: it is the gift of God: not of works, lest any man should boast."

Another verse that gave me hope was Rom. 6:23, "For the wages of sin is death, but the gift of God is eternal life through Jesus Christ our Lord." I knew that we all die someday, no matter how good or bad, sick or healthy, rich or poor we have been. I knew in my heart that God's promises of eternal salvation were what really counted. I knew that, and yet I still wanted to be healed on earth. Sometimes, like Job, I cried out, "Why me, God?"

Going back to the rehab center after weekends with Tom and my friends was always hard. My favorite times were bedtime and rest time. These were my hours to daydream, to leave the world of reality and the nightmare I was living. I would let my mind drift back into the past when I was normal and healthy and could walk and run. But when I awoke, everything was the same.

"How did I get into this mess? What did I eat? Was it that swine flu shot? Why did I get it?" Over and over again I would torture myself, trying to figure out what I could have done to avoid my situation.

Eventually I stopped blaming myself. I had done what I thought was right at the time. I grew to accept that, and tried to learn to be content in my circumstances.

Then one night everything fell down around me again. Joyce had been discharged, and my new roommate, Dorothy, was a sweet 70-year-old woman who couldn't talk. Her family showed her so much love and respect that I knew Dorothy had to be a very special person. She had suffered a stroke that destroyed her speech and paralyzed one side of her body.

Bob and Charlene arrived about 7:30 that night, cheerful and smiling. They greeted Dorothy and me.

"How was your week?" Charlene wanted to know. We prayed

82

together, and Bob gave a mini-sermon. I felt so fortunate to have my own private worship services every Friday. They prayed for the severe depression I had been experiencing since the return of the weakness.

Talking with them always helped me see how relevant the Scriptures are to life today.

I had an uneasy feeling when they were about to leave.

"Don't leave. Hide under my bed and stay tonight," I said, only half joking. My voice was weak.

"You'll be fine, Carol," Charlene said. "The psalmist said, 'he shall give his angels charge over thee, to keep thee in all thy ways.' Believe that," she reassured me.

After they left I tried to sleep. A heavy, anxious feeling filled me.

About 10 p.m., I felt my throat closing in again, and I began gasping for air. I struggled to fill my lungs, only to feel that they weren't getting enough oxygen. I fought down panic.

"Dorothy, Dorothy, I can't breathe," I whispered to my roommate. I couldn't yell; my throat muscles were too weak.

Dorothy tried to ring her call bell. It wouldn't work! I tried to ring mine, and it didn't work either. I couldn't move to get out of bed. Neither could Dorothy. Neither of us could yell for a nurse. I was afraid I would die of suffocation.

"Oh, Lord, help me. Protect me. I do want to live," I pleaded.

God used Dorothy, helpless as she was, to save my life. She managed to grab a spoon that was on her bedside table, and with her one good hand, she pounded on the table.

Trapped in my bed, I gasped for air as Dorothy pounded on the table. It seemed like she pounded for an hour, but it couldn't have been that long. Because many of the patients were confused, there often was a lot of yelling and pounding going on.

What a relief when a nurse came in to check, and I mouthed, "I can't breathe." Then, relieved and exhausted, I drifted off into unconsciousness.

The next thing I knew, the lights were on and I was hooked

up to an oxygen tank. Four or five nurses were standing around my bed.

If they hadn't acted as quickly as they did, I would have passed away during the night. The thing I had feared most, respiratory failure, had happened.

The nurses left the lights on and wouldn't let me go back to sleep; they were afraid I would die.

An ambulance later arrived and I was carefully moved from my bed to a stretcher for an emergency trip that would take me back to the hospital.

I looked at Dorothy and thought, *Thank you*. She was crying. Dorothy was an angel for me that dangerous night.

The ride was swift, the siren was running the entire time, and I was hooked up to a portable oxygen tank. I had heard ambulances wailing many times, but I had never been in one.

After spending $3\frac{1}{2}$ months in the rehabilitation center, leaving by emergency ambulance was a terrible disappointment. Besides my fear, I felt a deep sadness that I wasn't walking out and going home.

My neurologist had been following my case the whole time while I was at the rehab center, and he was waiting at the hospital. He wanted to perform emergency surgery for a tracheostomy. I didn't want a trach. I hated having a hole in my throat and not being able to talk to anyone. I felt certain I would be all right now that I was back in the hospital and could have oxygen if I needed it. I was breathing easier already.

"Carol, you have to have a trach. You need one, and you need one now," he insisted. "You could have respiratory failure again."

I wouldn't listen to him. I felt more secure in the hospital, and knew that I could be hooked up to a respirator if necessary. I was afraid another trach would be permanent, and I didn't want a permanent tube in my throat—or another scar. Tom agreed with my wishes.

84

My doctor was furious. He insisted that we see a psychiatrist. Tom and I were quite upset at the suggestion.

Unwillingly, we talked to the psychiatrist. We told him we felt God had protected me so far and wouldn't let me die now. I hated having a trach and we just didn't think that I really needed another one. He tried to convince us to change our minds, but we refused.

His report stated that we were mentally competent, but he felt we were making a mistake. My doctor said he didn't understand our reasoning, but he couldn't give me a trach if I refused.

I was breathing easier; the oxygen I had received seemed to help relax and loosen my throat muscles, so Tom went home that evening. About 4 a.m. I awoke in the intensive care unit, unable to utter a sound. I couldn't move anything except my eyes. That quickly, paralysis had struck again. I realized then how wrong I had been to refuse the trach. God works through doctors, and I hadn't been willing to listen when my doctor said something I didn't want to hear. My will had overruled my common sense again.

A nurse came to check me, and I mouthed "Trach, trach," to her. Each breath was a terrible struggle. Again, I felt close to death.

Now that I desperately wanted a trach, I couldn't have one. My blood pressure had dropped dangerously, and I couldn't have the operation.

A doctor came into the room and ordered a respirator.

"Lower the head of her bed," he directed the nurse. "That will help stabilize her blood pressure."

A thick tube was forced down my nose and throat. All of a sudden I could breathe, but it hurt terribly. My weakened lungs weren't used to being expanded, and the respirator was doing my breathing for me. The pain was unbearable, and I longed for a trach. At least that didn't hurt as much.

I watched the cylinder on the respirator go up and down as it breathed for me. Despite the terrible pain, it was a relief to get oxygen in my lungs. The respirator tube made my nose and throat feel raw, and there wasn't much the nurses could do except spray my throat with antiseptic.

I didn't want anyone to touch me, turn me, or even brush my hair because I was in so much pain. I wanted everyone to leave me alone.

The next several days were hazy. I remember Tom and my dad sort of floating in and out of the room. Then I saw my sister Diane come in. She came over to my bedside. I saw that her eyes were red and puffy. .

Why would Diane fly all the way from Texas? One by one, all my family members arrived. They couldn't all come in the room at once, but they took turns staying with me. I knew then something was seriously wrong.

I looked at Tom in fear.

"It's OK, Carol, you'll be OK," he reassured me.

Later, I found out that the doctors didn't think I would survive. I had grown very weak and thin, and they didn't think I had the strength to pull out of it.

Theresa and Tom sat up with me that entire weekend and waited through the crisis. All night long, every night, they were there.

I looked up at Theresa and mouthed, "I am going to die."

Her eyes filled with tears and she said, "Stop it. I won't stay in this room if you talk like that. You promised me when I saw you last that you would never give up hope."

Her love gave me strength. I met her eyes, and I mouthed, "I will try."

Tom called Charlene to come to the hospital. Charlene said later that Tom had explained in a low voice, "They aren't giving Carol very long to live."

Charlene began to pray, binding the devil in Jesus' name. By this time, my bed was tipped so that I was completely upside down. The doctors came in again and motioned Tom outside the room. Tom motioned Charlene outside, too.

The nurses became upset because my family and Charlene insisted on being with me. They wanted me to be as quiet and protected as possible, but my family didn't want me to be alone.

Charlene said later that while the medical personnel were giving Tom coffee and trying to prepare them for my death, she "got her spiritual dander up" and came back into my room. As she explains it, I was still upside down and connected to the respirator, but I wasn't responding. Charlene got down on her knees and put her head beside my ear.

"Trust him, Carol, he will protect you," she whispered. "I'm not talking to you, Carol, I'm speaking to your spirit. In the name of Jesus Christ of Nazareth I rebuke and bind every spirit of death and I say, Carol, live in the name of Jesus. In the name of Jesus, live!"

I couldn't respond to Charlene's words, but I heard them. She went on and whispered many healing verses into my ear. " 'The very God of peace sanctify you wholly; and I pray God your whole spirit and soul and body be preserved blameless unto the coming of our Lord Jesus Christ,' " she quoted (1 Thess. 5:23).

Those healing Scriptures Charlene had memorized and which came back to her then were a lifeline for me. I began to feel that I could hold onto life. . . . My blood pressure began to stabilize, and the nurse raised the head of my bed to a horizontal position.

Although my condition was better, I was still too sick to communicate much. Heavily medicated for pain, I wasn't very alert. I opened my eyes from time to time and looked around to see the worried faces of my family. Then my eyes would drop shut again.

The doctors told my family that the next few days would be critical. I made it through the first critical 24 hours, and the doctors gave me another 24 hours, then another.

Tom didn't leave the hospital. For a whole week he slept in the lobby in his clothes. I had my own private nurse, because I was hooked up to machines and couldn't talk or move. I had no way to communicate.

The next days were pain-filled and agonizing. I became terribly discouraged again. The tube in my nose and throat hurt badly. My lungs ached with every breath the respirator took, but I was dependent on it for my life.

Through everything so far, I had wanted to live. Now I understood how Job felt when he wished he had never been born. When the pain was the most excruciating, I looked at my poor husband sitting at my bedside and thought, "What did he do to deserve all this? What did I do?" Several times I begged him to take my life and end our misery, mouthing, "Kill me, kill me."

I really didn't want him to kill me, because then he would be in trouble, but I couldn't stand the pain. I was getting as many pain shots as I could have, but they didn't help enough. I wanted the Lord to take me home.

When I was a little girl, there were only two things I was afraid of: death and childbirth. Now death would have been a welcome relief.

Where was my faith? It was there, and the Lord had a tight hold of my hand. I know he carried me through this terrible time. The prayers of my family and friends sustained me.

"Jesus, please take me home," I begged. If I wasn't going to be healed instantly, I wanted nothing more to do with this pain-filled world. A verse I had read and memorized came to mind: "If thou shalt confess with thy mouth the Lord Jesus, and shalt believe in thine heart that God hath raised him from the dead, thou shalt be saved" (Rom. 10:8-9). "I believe in you, Lord Jesus; please take me home," I prayed over and over.

My dad came to visit me, bringing a Christian friend with him. The two brought a vial of oil along so that they could anoint me. Dad said the glass bottle had dropped on the steps outside the hospital, but hadn't broken. His friend poured the oil on me and prayed for me.

Instead of dying, I became a little bit stronger. By the end of the week, I was so hungry that my nurse tried to feed me some strained soup. I was on IVs, but they aren't very filling. More of the food came out my nose than went down my throat. Trying to eat caused more secretions, and the tube I breathed with kept getting plugged. I managed to swallow a few mouthfuls, and then had to stop because I was exhausted.

That night I felt like I was suffocating again. I tried to tell Tom.

Rolling my eyes toward the machine, I mouthed, "I can't breathe."

Tom went into the hall and found a nurse. "Carol can't breathe," he told her. "Help us."

Several times he asked for help, but each time the nurses checked the machine, found nothing wrong, and then left. The machine seemed to be working, but I was still struggling for breath. What we didn't know then was that the doctors had written in my report, "prognosis poor." They didn't really expect me to live.

My nurse friend Linda came to sit with me when she was off duty. She and Tom stayed by my side. A few minutes before Tom had to leave, I struggled as hard as I could for air, but could get none at all. Everything went black.

According to Tom, I began turning blue. Linda tore out of the room.

"Get in here. Carol is in trouble," she yelled.

The R.N. ran into my room, disconnected the respirator and manually pumped air into my lungs through the ET tube with a small plastic bag.

I opened my eyes and couldn't figure out what was going on. Someone wheeled in another respirator, and they hooked me up again. I was so dizzy that I couldn't comprehend what happened. I must have mouthed, "What happened?" to Tom fifty times.

"Your respirator wasn't working right. You couldn't get air and passed out. They got a new respirator," he explained patiently each time I asked.

I couldn't relate to anything in the room. I couldn't understand what I was doing in a hospital bed. Over and over, Tom explained things to me.

Had I passed out ten minutes later, after Tom had gone home and Linda had left, I don't know if I would have survived.

My doctor told me later that these machines rarely malfunction. But in my case it did.

I grew even weaker. Even opening my eyes was too much effort. My prognosis was no longer "poor," now it was "grave."

My blood pressure had stabilized enough that I could be given another trach, and I wanted one. Tom and I had told the doctors earlier to give me a trach as soon as possible. An ET tube cannot be left in a patient's nose very long or infection may set in. I was relieved when they finally pulled the tube out. The thought of another scar didn't bother me much anymore. I just wanted to be rid of the pain of the ET tube. My doctors had hoped I would improve to the point where they could pull the tube out and not have to give me a trach, but that didn't happen.

So two weeks after I left the rehab center by ambulance, I had surgery for another tracheostomy. Charlene was there again, praying me through the turmoil. My family began their vigil once more. At this point, I was completely paralyzed, able only to open and close my eyes.

That was all I could do—open and close my eyes. Was this it? After all our prayers and struggles, was I to end up with a permanent tracheostomy, as the doctors suggested, living in a nursing home? How much more of this could I expect Tom to endure? How much more could *I* endure?

8

I WAS FEELING GOOD AND SORRY for myself. I had been sick for so long, and all my friends and family were at least an hour's drive away. When they did visit, I couldn't talk to them because of my tracheostomy. Depression plagued me again, and I was often angry inside.

I had become dependent on my trach, which was now hooked up to a respirator. I felt uneasy even at the thought of breathing on my own, because my lungs had stopped working before and I was afraid they might stop again.

It was autumn, and I was lying in a hospital bed staring at the ceiling. I always enjoy autumn, with the leaves in their last colored glory, the crops ripe and ready for harvesting, and school classes going in full swing. I missed being in my classroom.

As I lay there immersed in self-pity, trying to relax and concentrate on breathing with the machine, I thought about Tom. He was going to be the best man in his friend's wedding, and many of our friends had been invited. I knew there would be a lot of single, attractive women at the big ceremony and celebration. I trusted Tom, but after all, he was a healthy, normal man. *He probably won't be able to help comparing me, wasted away and connected to tubes, with all the pretty girls at the wedding,* I thought. As much as I wanted to, I certainly hadn't been able to be much of a wife to him.

He's only human, I thought painfully, *What if he falls in love with someone else?*

But he loves me. He hasn't left me, even when I told him to, thank God, I reassured myself.

Tom had been so good to me through it all. Even when I told him to get out of my life, to divorce me because he deserved a better life, he didn't listen.

"I'm not going to leave you," he would say firmly. Subject closed.

But I knew that everyone has their limits. Before, we were hoping I would be walking by now. According to our doctors, though, I would probably always be in this condition. My faith and hopes for healing had sunk to an all-time low.

I should have been happy for Tom, that after all these months of drudgery he finally had a chance to celebrate and socialize. I just wanted so badly to be there with him. I felt like a little girl who isn't invited to the class party.

About 11 p.m. I heard footsteps, and my heart beat a little faster. I knew that walk. Tom slipped into my room, smiling and all dressed up in his tuxedo. He looked absolutely gorgeous.

He came up to my bed and looked down at me without a word. Then he just laid down beside me, tubes and all, and stayed with me for awhile.

Even though my trach made it impossible for me to speak, I tried to tell him with my eyes how much it meant to me that he would leave the wedding festivities and drive an hour to see me. I mouthed, "I love you so much."

He smiled and kissed me on the cheek.

Then he laughed. "Visiting hours are over, you know. I had to sneak up the back stairs."

Crazy, sweet Tom. I could just picture him sneaking up the

stairs in his tuxedo. He left to go home, and although I was still in pain, I felt good emotionally.

Tom wasn't one to say a lot, but his actions spoke for him. He was always there when I needed him, and he stuck by me without complaining. Where did he get his strength? Why wasn't our marriage cracking under the strain when so many others, even Christian marriages, were falling apart?

I decided that someday I would ask him to explain why he stuck by me even when I was willing to let him go. "Dear Lord, thank you so much for Tom," I prayed. I talked to the Lord a lot. Sometimes he must have wondered about my attitudes, but I knew he understood. As much as Tom and my family loved me, it was comforting to know that God loved me even more.

———◆———

Morris Cerullo, an evangelist with a healing ministry, had scheduled a crusade in Columbus for early October. Since I was still hooked up to the respirator, there was no way I could go. But Tom, Bob, Charlene, and my sisters Judy, Theresa, and Darlene went in my behalf.

I believed that the power of the Holy Spirit could be so strong in a body of believers, that miracles do occur. Despite all my setbacks and my faltering faith, I still believed in miracles.

Tom went forward when they asked for those who needed healing to come up for prayer. He wanted to be my intercessor.

Bob went backstage and talked with one of the ushers. "What more can we do?" he asked him. "We're praying and believing and asking God for a miracle. She's still critically ill."

The usher handed Bob cards with ten scripture verses printed on them.

"Have her read these verses three times a day and try to memorize them," he told Bob. "After each verse she should say, 'Jesus, I believe it; Jesus, I receive it; Jesus, I confess it.' "

After the crusade, Tom came to the hospital and told me about the verses. As he held the cards for me, I read them silently.

"I will take sickness away from the midst of thee" (Exod. 23:25). "And the prayer of faith shall save the sick, and the Lord shall raise him up" (James 5:15).

There were eight more healing verses. I read them all several times, and after each I repeated that I believed it, received it, and confessed it.

It made sense to me. The Bible says we should fill our mind with good thoughts and learn God's word. At different times I had already read and claimed many of these verses. I decided to really concentrate on memorizing and accepting what the verses said. Sometimes Charlene, Cynthia, or Katharina would read the verses aloud; sometimes I read them to myself.

The usher told Bob we should expect to see great things happen within ten days of reading the verses. Exactly ten days after I began reading the Scriptures, the doctors were able to unhook the respirator. They were amazed at my progress. Only three weeks before, they feared for my life. It had looked like I would be dependent on a respirator for life.

The caring, fatherly head of the respiratory department had begun turning the respirator down bit by bit so that my lungs would gradually take over. Each day he turned it down a little more. At the same time, I began moving my shoulders and pelvis a bit. Down, down went the respirator, from giving me 10 breaths a minute, to 8, to 3, and finally none. Then they turned it off completely for a few hours.

"I'm breathing alone!" I was scared, but excited. By the tenth day after I began reading the healing verses, I was completely weaned from the respirator.

My doctors were delighted. One medical report at this time read, "The recovery of respiratory function is encouraging." They decided I probably wouldn't have to live on a respirator. I could function without it, but I would have to have a permanent tracheostomy.

I didn't want that. "Lord, I don't want a pipe in my throat for the rest of my life," I prayed.

A few days later, the doctors said I was well enough that my hair could be washed. It hadn't been washed in nearly six weeks. I was thrilled to have shiny, clean hair again.

We kept praying, and I kept reading the healing Scriptures regularly. Exactly ten days after the respirator was turned off, the doctors took out my trach tube. I was breathing completely on my own!

My nurses sat me up in a chair, and I felt bright and peppy. I could move my shoulders and bottom a bit more.

"Quite spirited," read one doctor's report.

"Very encouraging," a lung specialist wrote.

My appetite rapidly returned once I was able to breathe and swallow again. I began eating baby food and soups. "I want a ham sandwich!" I declared one day, and the kitchen sent one right up. I ate it with relish and didn't choke a bit.

The kitchen staff sent one of their dieticians up to talk with me.

"Carol, we are so happy that you are finally eating again. You can order anything you want," she smiled.

After being their patient for a total of eight months, I was finally able to begin to enjoy real food again.

Pizza, my passion, was on the menu when Tom brought in a big one from Tiny's, a restaurant in Archbold known for their pizzas. Many times when I was unable to swallow, my mouth had watered just thinking about them.

The nurses heated the pizza in a microwave, and Tom and I attacked it with zest.

"Mmmmm, Tom, it's great!" I said with my mouth full.

I was making such rapid progress that everyone was amazed. My arms and legs were moving a little, and I was swallowing and breathing and talking easily.

I was so glad that I didn't have to have a permanent tracheostomy! I liked to talk, and I hated the idea of having a pipe in my throat forever. There would always be the danger of infection, as well.

About a week after the trach was removed, my doctors talked with me about my plans.

"Carol, we think you should go into a nursing home. You need 24-hour care, but you don't have to stay here in the hospital."

I didn't want to go to a nursing home. I wanted to go home. We all knew that I needed a lot of care, so Charlene called several dozen nurses who lived near our home and set up a round-the-clock schedule. The hospital staff helped us arrange rental of a hydraulic lift and a hospital bed. We borrowed a wheelchair and bedpan and were ready for my new life at home.

I was going home again! After being in hospitals for nearly a year, it was great to be heading for home. True, I wasn't walking home as I had planned, but at least I was alive. And my progress strengthened my determination to get well. I continued reading my healing verses and praying for a miracle.

Now another type of struggle began. After the initial excitement of being at home subsided a bit, I began to wonder if our marriage could survive my constant need for care, plus the total lack of privacy. We were never alone.

Tom was a great help to me, but he couldn't do everything. He worked long hours and needed his sleep.

"Can a man who changes his wife's bedpan ever see her as a mystery again?" I wondered.

I could tell that some of the things he had to do for me weren't pleasant, but he did them anyway.

I became sort of a community project. One of my day nurses, Linda, lived in Adrian, Michigan, and couldn't always make it in. Then ladies from the area would volunteer to come in. Charlene, Gert, Carol Hackett, and Mary Ellen were my most regular volunteers, although many women donated their time and care.

Charlene became like a mother to me. The Lord brought her into my life when I most needed a mother. She helped us in so many ways, from getting groceries for us to praying with us. She cleaned my house, fed me, did therapy, changed bedpans, and was always there when we needed her. Many days she spent more hours at my house than at hers. She would come anytime I needed her, day or night. Her fellowship was always a spiritual boost. Much of the time Charlene left her own daughters to be by my side.

"Charlene, you're so good to help me," I told her. "Your own family must miss you when you're here so much."

"They stick together and help each other out. Bob and I grounded the girls in the Scripture according to Prov. 22:6 that says, 'Train up a child in the way he should go: and when he is old, he will not depart from it.' They are doing OK, and they are praying for you, too," she explained.

Charlene wasn't the type of Christian who gushingly said, "I'll pray for you, dear" and went on her way. I didn't meet many of those, but I know they exist. She prayed for me and helped me in practical ways. I couldn't help thinking that that was what Jesus would have done.

I was gradually gaining strength, and I could even roll over in bed by December. When Theresa, my sister, offered to stay with us during her holiday break, we were really glad. She lived with us all of December, so we didn't need any other help during that time.

We had to chuckle a few times when she gave me the bedpan. She wasn't trained in nursing skills, and she would sometimes give it to me backwards.

"Hey, what's going on? That hurts!" I would complain. Then Theresa would check and discover her mistake.

We laughed. I am such a modest person that I hated having to use a bedpan. But I learned to grin and bear it.

Theresa washed my hair by putting a bucket on my lap and wheeling me to the kitchen sink. Using the spray hose, she soaped and rinsed my hair. More often than not, she got just as wet as I did.

Theresa was good to me, but I wasn't always pleasant to her. It seems that so often we take out our fears and frustrations on those closest to us. Sometimes, if things weren't done just right or I was uncomfortable, I would snap at Theresa. Once I told her to go home.

My words and attitude must have hurt my sister deeply, but she didn't leave. She just stayed and helped as much as she could, cheering us up with her sense of humor.

One night everything got to me again. I was tired of being a prisoner in my own home. I was tired of being a burden to Tom and Theresa. I thought everyone was asleep, and I cried and cried.

Theresa told me later that she heard me crying, and was terribly worried. She stayed awake, listening to make sure I was all right, until I dropped off to sleep.

Tom helped us as much as he could, but he was working 12-hour shifts. The hours were hard on him, but we needed the money. We were so thankful that he had a job. His days consisted of work, sleep, visiting and helping me, and more work—not a very exciting life.

Theresa did have one fault. She was as afraid of mice as I was. One evening as we relaxed in the living room, a tiny mouse scurried across the floor.

"Oh, Theresa, run and get a mousetrap, please?" I begged her. "What if he crawls up on my bed tonight?"

She pulled her feet up onto the couch. "No way. I'm not walking across this room," she declared. And no amount of begging or bribery could change her mind. We both knew it was silly, but the tiny creature enjoyed his freedom until Tom returned home later that night.

My good friend Linda, the nurse, and her husband Butch brought me a "standing box" one afternoon. By gripping the edges of this box, I was able to stand alone. I stood as long as I could, then sat back down.

At first I could only stand a few seconds, but gradually I built my time up to a half hour. This gave me tremendous hope, and I felt certain that I was on my way to recovery.

Two weeks before Christmas, my sister Judy, her husband Les, and their daughter Holly came to visit. It was great to see them, and as we were catching up on everything, Pat and Jean, my therapists from the rehab center, pulled in the driveway.

They were amazed to see me eating alone. The last time they had seen me, I was in respiratory failure. By leaning back against the bed and resting my arm on my chest, I could awkwardly hold a sandwich and eat it alone. I still couldn't grip silverware, but I was sure that would come.

The Christmas season meant even more to me than usual, because I was at home with Tom. I was thankful to be breathing on my own.

"Last Christmas, I had a trach," I recalled. "This year I can wish my friends a Merry Christmas."

Tom bought me an exercise bike for Christmas, and he said he expected me to be using it soon.

What I wasn't telling anyone besides Tom was that I felt another relapse coming on. I could always tell when they started. My fingers tingled, I felt weaker, and swallowing and breathing became more difficult. The doctors were right. I would struggle hard to improve, only to suffer a relapse. The decline dimmed some of the joy of the season for me.

Relentlessly, the decline continued, weakening my muscles. January is often a gray, depressing month in Ohio, and I felt myself slipping, physically and emotionally. I became as gloomy as the weather.

The next few months were a period of stability, although once again I completely lost the use of my arms and legs. I couldn't move or stand anymore. My swallowing remained the same; we had asked a local chiropractor to help me with that.

I hadn't given up my desire for a miracle. One day Tom, Charlene, Katharina, Barb Graf, and I drove to Akron for a healing service. Ernest Angley, an evangelist, was speaking. Many people with severe handicaps of all kinds were there, all hoping for a miracle. So was I.

Again, God didn't heal me instantly. We drove home down-hearted.

"God will heal you, Carol. He will," Charlene told me, noticing my silence.

"I know. I just wanted it to happen today," I replied.

Margie received a letter from Darlene about this time:

Carol is the same—no arm or leg movement. She gets very depressed at times, but overall has an amazingly good attitude. . . . Tom is holding up very well. Carol has been reading more books on miracles and attended a faith healing service in Akron.

I could read books by sitting at the kitchen table in my wheel-chair, turning the pages with my mouthstick. I also had a big Bible to read from. God's promises kept me going.

After Theresa went back to college, we hired nurses again, though only for the times when Tom was at work. He took care of me when he was at home.

Most of my nurses and aides were Christians. Their fellowship was a tremendous blessing to me.

We had some good laughs. Once when one of my aides, Barb, was giving me a foul-tasting laxative, she read the label aloud: "I don't know, Carol, this label says, 'No burn, no gripe,' but you sure gripe when you have to take it!" We cracked up, laughing, because it was so true.

Helen Weldy, a counselor at the high school who had been a home economics teacher when I was doing my student teaching, became a close friend. I was touched but not surprised when she showed up at my house with a pattern book and asked me to select some patterns I liked.

It was so like Helen to think of something like making new clothes for me. She sewed some attractive wraparound skirts and blouses that were fastened with Velcro. I was hard to dress, and these clothes were easy for my nurses to slip on and off me.

I wore my new wardrobe all the time. I loved it, and felt better about my appearance.

I'm convinced that a sense of humor is God's special gift to help us through tough times. Proverbs 17:22 says, "A merry heart doeth good like a medicine." The times I could laugh heartily were wonderful medicine for me, and they seemed to help balance the times when I cried too much.

My sister Margie and her little girls Faith and Catherine flew in from the Virgin Islands to visit us. Seeing her again brought back delightful memories of happier days.

We made popcorn one afternoon, and I was eating it in my normal fashion, by leaning down from the wheelchair to the bowl on the kitchen table, picking up a piece or two with my lips, and then sitting up and chewing it. No one had to feed me, and it tasted just as good that way.

Faith, Margie's four-year-old, watched me stick my head in my bowl and evidently decided it looked like fun. When I looked over at her, she had her head in the bowl, eating just like Aunt Carol ate.

I thought it was pretty comical. "Margie, look!" I laughed.

Poor Margie was a bit embarrassed, afraid that I might be hurt that Faith was imitating me. But it was such a sight, me eating with my head in the bowl out of necessity, and little Faith innocently imitating me, that we all laughed.

During April, May, and June, I was pretty stable. I ate whatever I wanted to, and was breathing just fine. Our life settled into a routine. I was still a quadriplegic, but life wasn't bad. My nurses took good care of me, and Tom and I had some time alone to finally have a semblance of a marriage.

At least now we could talk about private things and hold each other and share little things. Our relationship was a far cry from what I had always dreamed of, and our physical relationship was certainly very limited.

I did have feeling in all parts of my body, even though I was paralyzed. Sometimes the feeling was one of hypersensitivity, especially in my hands and feet. People who assume that the handicapped are doomed to a life without intimacy are wrong. Granted, our love life wasn't the same as it was on our honeymoon. But as long as two people love each other, they can have a close, intimate relationship.

I was so much in love with Tom. Sometimes I would watch him as he walked around the house or was engrossed in a TV show, and just thank God for giving me that wonderful man

Still, we had our conflicts. Sometimes he would yell at me in frustration, or I would cry and feel sorry for myself. We had tempers, and we reacted in very human ways when the frustrations of quadriplegia became too much for us.

Some encounters would go like this:

"Tom, could I have some juice?"

"Tom, my nose itches."

"Tom, could you please move my leg? It hurts."

"Carol, do you need something *all* the time?"

Then I would be hurt and cry and he would stomp off, telling me to stop having a pity party. We always made up soon after, and we actually got along amazingly well, considering that Tom had never intended to be a nurse, and I wasn't the type who enjoyed lying around.

Tom rarely cried. But one night as I rested in the hospital bed in the living room, we both wept because it was just so hard.

This was the first time I had known just how difficult things were for Tom. He kept a lot inside so that his family and I wouldn't worry about him.

We both just sobbed. I said a few words, pouring my heart out, and then sobbed again. He did the same.

"I'm sorry, Tom," I cried.

"It's . . . not your fault," he sobbed.

"I wish."

"I know."

"I love you."

"I love you, too."

We cried together for an hour straight. I felt even closer to my husband than before.

Tom never laid any guilt on my shoulders about the money or my helplessness. He never said, "We could have so much more or do so many things but we can't because you're too sick and we don't have any money." Not once did he make me feel guilty.

When I thought about how some of my friends' husbands got mad at them for spending too much money, I knew how lucky I was to have Tom. I was spending *a lot* more money than they were, yet he didn't complain.

9

SPRING AND SUMMER ARE LOVELY in Ohio. Sometimes I would sit in the wheelchair in our yard and enjoy the flowers, birds, and sun on my body. Even the annoying mosquitoes, which I couldn't swat, couldn't keep me indoors.

Although I was still pretty helpless, I had been much worse, and I thanked God every day for letting me be at home. I was still praying for a miracle and trying to trust God.

Then in August, a nagging thought in the back of my mind grew stronger and stronger until I couldn't keep it to myself any longer. I didn't want to worry Tom, so I confided in Charlene.

"I think I'm pregnant!" I blurted.

Shocked, she tried to reassure me. "Carol, I doubt it. Your chances of conceiving are very small. It's nearly impossible. Our bodies can play tricks on us."

Considering our nearly nonexistent sex life, and my condition, it *was* almost impossible. But not completely.

"But Charlene, I've missed three periods in a row," I said.

"I'm sure you're not pregnant. Lots of things can cause missed periods. But I'll get a test for you just to put your mind at ease," she offered.

Although I love children and had always wanted a family, I was harder to care for than a baby. A pregnancy now would be a disaster.

Charlene sent my urine sample to the doctor's office. All day I waited, anxiously, one moment certain that I wasn't pregnant, the next worried sick that I was.

"Oh, Lord, whatever will we do? Not now, Lord, please. Please don't let me be pregnant," I pleaded.

Yet even as I prayed, I knew that what was done, was done. If I was pregnant, I was pregnant.

Charlene came over later that day.

"Carol, the test was positive. It looks like you're going to have a baby. Dr. Thompson will come over to examine you." She hugged me close.

I was stunned, unable to think straight.

Tom had to be told, of course. Never have I seen such a mixture of shock and anguish on a face.

"No. Are you sure?" he said.

Poor Tom. Patient and strong, he had put up with my condition for so long. And we, of all people, ended up with a pregnancy.

How could Tom, strong as he was, possibly handle two helpless human beings? I weighed only 95 pounds, and Tom could lift me, but I was hard-to-handle deadweight. My arms and legs dangled at my sides, uncontrollable. Getting through doorways was quite a trick.

We talked to several doctors about our baby. I was worried that the child would be paralyzed or abnormal.

"Of course, only God knows if the baby will be completely normal," one doctor said. "But your baby has as much a chance as any of being normal. The disease is not hereditary."

Anxiety still plagued me. How could my weak and skinny body nourish a child? What would people say? Wouldn't everyone think we were selfish to have a child when I couldn't take proper care of it?

My doctors spoke privately with Tom about the possibility of an abortion.

"We're not sure what triggers Carol's relapses, but she nearly died with the last bad one. Having a baby could kill her," Dr. Thompson told Tom. "As the child grows in the uterus, it could press on Carol's lungs. With her history of breathing problems, it could be dangerous." He paused, then went on reluctantly. "A termination would be the best thing for Carol."

Other doctors felt the same way. Tom told me what the doctors had said.

"I don't want you to die," he said.

"But we can't kill our baby!" I cried. "God wouldn't have let me get pregnant if I shouldn't have this baby. And why should he ever heal me if I kill the baby?"

"I know. I know how you feel. But I don't want to lose you," he said quietly. "I have mixed emotions."

Tom didn't believe in abortion, either. When one life is endangered by another, though, you question many things you never had to question before.

We decided to just keep on trusting God with my life, and take one day at a time. He had brought me safely through the valley of the shadow of death many times, and I knew he wouldn't fail me now.

"We want to have this baby. No abortion," Tom told the doctors. They were concerned, but respected our decision.

"OK. We'll do our best to save them both," Dr. Thompson said.

Despite my knowledge that God was in control, I did worry. I kept wondering how we could handle a baby, and how my system could take a pregnancy.

"Remember, Carol, day by day. Trust the Lord," Charlene would encourage me.

Although the people of our community were loving and concerned, as in all small towns, sometimes discussion can turn into gossip and rumors. I was afraid of what people would say about me being pregnant, so I decided to keep it a secret for as long as possible. Only a few people knew.

I often felt worthless and guilty. My mind was trapped in my body, my *pregnant* body. Sometimes, with help from my nurses, I balanced our checkbook, paid bills, and did whatever other mental work I could to help Tom and feel useful.

On the weekends, Tom cared for me by himself. We often played chess. Although I couldn't move the pieces, I could tell him where to move mine. I became pretty adept at planning strategies, and we had a lot of fun. Mary Ellen usually stopped in on Sundays to see if we needed anything.

Tom fed me, brushed my teeth, gave me the bedpan, cooked, and made me as comfortable as possible. He wasn't too good at doing my hair, but he did his best. I often wore my trusty blue and gold high-top tennis shoes. Blue and gold were our school colors and the University of Michigan colors, so I got a lot of ribbing about having the old school spirit. Because I was from Ohio, and Ohio State University and the University of Michigan football teams were rivals, I was also teased about wearing the wrong colors! I couldn't win.

By taking one day at a time, Tom and I were able to cope with our almost overwhelming situation. I even grew excited once in awhile at the thought of a child, half mine and half Tom's, yet a new person.

The first time the baby kicked was an awesome experience, as it is for almost all first-time mothers. My eyes filled with tears.

"Tom. Feel," I whispered the next time it happened.

He put his hand on my belly and felt the little flutter inside. His face softened. I think both of us experienced a big change that day. This really was a new person, created in the image of God, growing inside me.

I read Psalm 139, and it had fresh meaning: "For thou didst form my inward parts, thou didst knit me together in my mother's womb. I praise thee, for thou art fearful and wonderful. Wonderful are thy works! Thou knowest me right well; my frame was not hidden from thee, when I was being made in secret, intricately wrought in the depths of the earth. Thy eyes beheld my unformed substance; in thy book were written, every one of them, the days that were formed for me, when as yet there was none of them" (RSV).

I knew that God had planned this child, and for whatever reason, we would have to trust him to see us through this. "Trust the Lord with all thy heart, and lean not to thine own understanding," was my special verse, and I tried to do just that.

———————◆———————

In September, Tom and I drove to Dayton for an Oral Roberts healing service. We stopped at my sister Darlene's home to visit. Another of my sisters, Judy, was there with her husband Les and their two girls.

I hadn't seen Les in months, and he was painfully thin. He looked exhausted.

"Judy, what's wrong with Les?" I asked her as soon as we were alone.

"Please, Carol, let's not talk about it when he's around. It'll just make him feel worse," she said.

I knew that Les had been born with a liver abnormality, and he had to keep close watch on it. He was on medication. He had always looked strong and healthy before, though. I was really worried about him.

Darlene, Tom, and I drove to the service. I wanted an instant miracle, and I prayed for Les, too. I really tried to believe unflinchingly, but I wasn't healed. Tom, Darlene, and I all cried. We were so disappointed. The counselors at the service promised us that I would get well, but that it could take years. They said to keep believing. I already knew that. I wanted a miracle.

We headed for home again, with me just as paralyzed as

before. I still felt that God could and would heal me complete-ly, and I was leaving no stone unturned. I just wasn't sure when or how he would heal me.

During October, I grew weaker again. The little strength I had seemed to ebb away, and I slept a lot. Members of a nearby Mennonite church began bringing supper to our home every Saturday night. We really appreciated the food. Tom wasn't too happy about cooking for us.

Tom and I spent a quiet Thanksgiving at home. It was such a production to take me anywhere, with the wheelchair and bedpan and all. It was much more restful to stay home.

I wanted the baby to be as healthy as possible, so I had been taking a lot of vitamins. As I grew weaker, and started choking again, it was impossible to swallow them, so I had to stop.

Janis Watson, a neighbor, prepared custard for me several times a week. My nurses and friends fed me as much of this as I could eat, as well as pureed peaches, pears, and plums.

My visiting nurse was concerned that the baby wasn't getting enough nutrition, so she brought me some capsule vitamins that could be broken open and stirred into my food. My guardian angels—those dear women and Christian friends who came and cared for me—made it possible for Tom to keep his job, and for our baby to be nourished.

Janis, Charlene, and another teacher friend, Carol Hackett, made homemade soups for me, which they thinned and sieved to remove all the little lumps. Even the tiniest speck made me choke. Whoever was feeding me had to warm up the soup over and over because it took so long to get any down my throat. Often, I just ate the soup cold.

One day Janis asked, "Wouldn't you like to get a microwave, Carol?"

I said, "Well, I doubt if Tom would want to buy one," and we dropped the subject. I knew that a microwave would have been a big help to both of us, but it was out of the question.

A few weeks later, a big box arrived on our doorstep. To my

shock, it was a microwave oven. Russ and Janis, out of the goodness of their hearts, had bought one for us as a Christmas gift.

"Janis, you shouldn't have done that," I protested.

"You two need it. You can get your soups heated quickly now, and Tom can make himself some food in it, too. It will save everyone time and work. And God has been good to us. We wanted to share," she smiled.

That microwave was a tremendous help to us. We had no idea how much we would use it until we had it.

Eating was such a chore that I would much rather have not eaten at all. But I also knew that I was eating for two, so I made myself choke down as much as possible. I didn't want to go back to the hospital until I had to.

"If I can just keep breathing and swallowing, I can nourish the baby," I thought, "and I won't have to go back into the hospital yet."

I wanted to stay at home as long as possible. I had a strong fear that if I were again hooked up to a respirator or lost consciousness, I might have to lose my baby. The fear was probably irrational, but somehow I felt that the longer I could stay at home, the better it would be for the baby and me.

Feeding me became a full-time process. Friends, family members, and neighbors took turns spooning soups, fruits, and custards into me. It was hard to remember that I had been gulping down sandwiches only a few weeks before.

Swallowing was my main concern. Throat massages, regular treatments by Dr. Targonski, a local chiropractor, and prayer kept my throat muscles relaxed enough to swallow.

Every Sunday, Ruth, my mother-in-law, came over to feed me and her future grandchild. She spent the entire day with us, because it took all day to get enough food into me.

Tom rarely let on that he was worried, but sometimes he couldn't keep it inside.

"Carol, how are we going to care for this baby?" he asked one day, quite upset. "I have my hands full with you!"

"Let's just not worry about the future. The Bible says not to be anxious about tomorrow, because each day's trouble is sufficient. So let's take it one day at a time," I said, repeating the comforting words Charlene had often said to me. "The Lord has given us this baby. I don't know how things will work out, but they will. We are going to manage."

We tried to remind ourselves of Phil. 4:13: "I can do all things through Christ which strengtheneth me."

Carol Hackett made some colorful posters and pinned them up in our living room. My favorite one read, "The Lord is the strength of my life, who shall I fear?"

"Carol, this baby is going to be a miracle baby. God has a purpose for everything, and this child will bless you and Tom," Charlene said one day.

I believed that, but I must admit that it was pretty hard for Tom and I to understand God's timing. We both still firmly believed I would be healed, but it was certainly taking a lot longer than we had ever anticipated.

I felt that I was better off staying at home than going to the hospital, as long as I could get enough nourishment for the baby. I realize now that I should probably have gone to the hospital as soon as the swallowing problems began. I just thank God that he protects us during our foolish times. Sometimes he must just shake his head at our stubbornness.

Because I needed to keep track of my weight for the doctors, Tom and I had to figure out a way to weigh me. I couldn't stand on the scales, and setting me on them didn't work. Finally Tom just picked me up, weighed us both, then set me down and weighed himself. By subtracting his weight from both our weights, we could keep track of my gains. Actually, it was kind of a fun way to be weighed.

Unfortunately, by Christmas I was too awkward and bulky to pick up and balance, so we stopped. I had gained only 12 pounds, and my tummy was pretty small.

"Well, Carol, most women have basketball stomachs when

they're pregnant," laughed Mary Ellen one day. "You've got a volleyball tummy."

I never did get to see my stomach sticking out in front of me, hiding my toes. Not once during my pregnancy could I stand up.

By the end of January, my throat muscles wouldn't work at all. No amount of patience, struggle, or tears could force anything down.

My baby wasn't due for another six weeks. I didn't want to spend all that time, plus recuperation time afterward, in the hospital away from Tom. I had no choice, though, if I wanted to survive. My visiting nurse made all the arrangements, and I checked into still another hospital, this one noted for its excellent high-risk pregnancy unit. As things turned out, it was a blessing that I went into the hospital when I did.

10

Now there were some new machines added to the ones I was accustomed to being hooked up to. They measured my baby's heartbeat and my contractions (I was having false labor). Because I was dehydrated, I was also hooked up to an IV.

I improved some when I was in the hospital, and my throat opened up a tiny bit. My doctors were considering putting still another tube into me to feed me, but I managed to get down some poached eggs, pureed fruits, and creamed soups, so they let me continue to eat alone.

"God, please feed this baby," I prayed daily. The wonder of new life growing within me was mixed with apprehension at the tremendous responsibility ahead. I did hope that the child was a boy, and that he would look like Tom.

As new life was growing within my body, the life of my brother-in-law, Les, had been ebbing away. When Tom told me in January that Les had died, I couldn't believe it. The family had been keeping his critical condition from me. He had been terribly ill for nearly a year, and they had sheltered me from knowing about it. I remembered how tired he had looked the last time I had seen him.

"Oh, Lord, no," I groaned, crying for my sister. Poor Judy—she was only 31, with two little girls to care for. Here the whole family had been so worried about *me*, but it was Les who was dying.

People can go so quickly. Sometimes those who seem healthy are sick and we don't even know it. I couldn't go to the funeral, but Judy came to see us soon after Les' death.

"Judy, I'm so sorry," I sobbed.

Judy was holding up well. *She* tried to console *me*, and said, "Les' suffering is over. He didn't get a physical healing, but he was spiritually healed. And now he has a glorified body. Carol, he was a Christian when he died."

Even though I grieved for Les, I rejoiced that he knew the Lord. Les' roommate in the hospital was a committed Christian, and he led both Les and Judy to a new commitment to the Lord.

Les' death was hard on me. My faith took a beating. I couldn't understand why a young father like him would die. I wondered if I would ever get a miracle to walk again. Why hadn't God healed Les?

Later I received a letter from Judy that helped me put things in perspective:

Praise God that soon we'll all be with him and never shed another tear nor feel any more pain. When I think of the house Les is building for me there right now, I get so excited I can hardly contain it. Studying has made it all so real to me; makes it easy to see. PTL. All our love, Judy and girls.

A few days after I was admitted to the hospital, my bag of waters ruptured. At first I didn't even know what had happened.

"Carol, we have to induce labor. The baby might be endangered by infection if we don't," my doctor said. He assured me that the child was large enough to survive, although it was five weeks early.

114

I was transferred to the OB unit, where Flo, the supervisor, and Fran, my nurse, immediately took me under their wings. I felt secure in their care.

"It'll be a boy," I joked with Fran. "He kicked so much, I think he has a football in there!"

"Have you named him?" she asked.

I smiled. "We like Jeffrey."

I wasn't smiling for long. The medication used to induce labor wasn't working. I was having real contractions, and they hurt, but I wasn't dilating enough for a normal birth.

My doctors were upset. They wanted me to have a natural childbirth.

"If we do surgery and take the baby with a cesarean section, it could be dangerous for you, Carol," explained my doctor. "As weak and paralyzed as you are, you could catch pneumonia. You have to have it naturally."

We tried, but my body wouldn't cooperate. Death and childbirth had always been my two biggest fears. I had faced and conquered one fear. Now it was time to face the other.

The baby was in more danger as time passed. I still wasn't dilating. The pain was terrible, so I received pain shots every few hours.

"Carol, the baby's heartbeat is strong. I don't think we can wait any longer. We're going to take it with a C-section," my doctor said.

I was glad. I was afraid I didn't have the strength to go through with natural childbirth. Besides, I had never had any classes in breathing, how to relax, or anything like that, although my sisters came to the hospital and gave me tips on how to have a baby naturally.

They rolled me down to surgery about 7 p.m. on February 6. When I looked around the room and saw all the doctors and nurses standing around me, I felt like I was in a TV doctor show.

The anesthetic began to take effect, and everything went fuzzy, then black.

Jeffrey was born at 7:32 p.m., February 6, 1980—healthy, hungry, and noisy. My obstetrician told Tom he had a healthy five-pound son and that I was fine.

My reserved, rock-like husband actually jumped up and down and ran down the hall in excitement, according to several reliable witnesses. He was beaming, proud and thrilled. Against so many odds, he was the father of a healthy child. Russ and Janis Watson, the Lantzes, and Tom were all laughing, crying, and hugging each other. "Praise the Lord!" rang out over and over.

This was really the first time that Tom had shown any happiness about the baby. He never said much before Jeff was born, because he didn't want to get my hopes up too much. I was delighted to hear of his reaction.

I finally recovered enough to see our son a few hours later. By then, Charlene had been on the phone, spreading the good news. Most of our friends and neighbors knew about Jeff before I did!

"Thank you, God," I breathed when I got the first glimpse of my little son. He was so delicate and perfect. I knew then that no matter how hard it was, we would somehow raise our child.

Although Jeff was born healthy, he wasn't out of danger. He couldn't digest his food properly, and I couldn't feed him, so he had to be fed through a tube in his nose.

"Poor little guy. Like mother, like son, I guess," I thought. Because he was premature, he was in an incubator. The nurse brought him in to see me often, and laid him on my chest so we could get to know each other.

"I'm your mommy, Jeffrey," I whispered, nuzzling his head. Now I had a new reason to walk again.

———◆———

We were showered with baby gifts. Jeff was probably the most "gifted" baby in the state. My friend Rita brought a whole pile of presents from members of St. Peter's Catholic Church. Several other area churches also had showers for us, and many friends brought gifts.

The gifts were a godsend, because we needed so many things for the baby. I had been too sick to shop, and Tom didn't know much about what babies need.

We kept praying that I would be healed enough to take care of Jeff and Tom. I knew that most of the doctors and nurses considered me a permanent quadriplegic, and things did look pretty hopeless. I had been quadriplegic for more than two years.

After Jeff was born, though, I thought, "This child is a miracle, and I'm not giving up now." James 5:15 says, "the prayer of faith shall save the sick, and the Lord shall raise him up." I believed and claimed that verse.

Several days after Jeff's birth, I moved my arms and legs a little bit. My body had released natural steroids, and they gave me strength.

"Tom! Watch!" I told him in excitement. It had been more than a year since I had moved so much. I was really happy because it gave me hope that the nerve damage wasn't permanent, after all. I still couldn't feed myself, but I was wiggling around pretty well.

By the time Jeff was a week old, I was eating soft eggs, ground meat, toast, and mashed potatoes again. After all those months of a liquid diet, I loved digging into regular food. I began to anticipate a rapid recovery.

Instead, I went into another decline. I also got the blues. I didn't want them, but there they were, dragging me down into depression. I knew that a lot of women have postpartum depression, but I didn't expect it, after all I had been through. I thought I was tougher than that.

Either Tom or friends slept by my bedside most of the nights I was in the hospital. Their presence reassured me. When Tom wasn't there, another Christian friend was, comforting me and praying with me.

The doctor's report at this time read, "Unfortunately, there is little hope for any improvement in her basic neurological status.

Tom and I were married on June 18, 1977, in a traditional church wedding. I was healthy, happy, and had a handsome husband. Life seemed perfect.

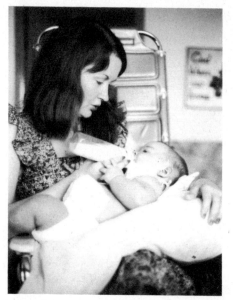

Little Jeffrey was my "miracle baby." Although I was in a wheelchair, I could feed him and talk to him.

At age 1½, Jeffrey loved the outdoors. Active and alert, he is our pride and joy.

. . . Continued psychological support and neurological monitoring are about all we have to offer."

I must have seemed uncooperative at times, but I was so weak that I couldn't always follow directions very well. Some of the tests the therapists gave me were too difficult for me to do. I just wanted to sleep.

I remembered how, when I had first gotten sick, I thought I would go to the hospital and the doctors would "fix" me. Now I realized that although doctors often are the instruments for God's healing, they can't always fix things. It was a rude awakening.

About 10 days after Jeff was born, I awoke about midnight, frightened. My lungs were congested, and it was hard to breathe again.

The nurses wanted to put a tube down my nose and throat to suction mucous out of my lungs. I couldn't talk, I could barely breathe, and I was afraid to go to sleep, afraid that I would never wake up.

I kept my mouth open, gasping for more air. I told the nurse to "call my husband, call my husband." I wanted Tom to come as soon as possible. I clearly remembered the agony of having a tube forced down my nose for the respirator, and I wanted no part of another one. I knew I was headed for respiratory failure, and the once-dreaded trach was what I wanted.

When Tom arrived, about 7 a.m., I was able to let him know that I wanted a trach. We asked for a doctor, and waited and waited. My breathing became more and more difficult, so I was given oxygen through my nose. Finally, a doctor came and ordered an IV. It took nearly two hours for the nurses and doctor to get an IV started. They had to stick me at least 15 times because my veins were too weak to handle the IV. Finally, they found one that was strong enough.

Then the doctor gave me a bronchoscopy to see what was causing my breathing problems. He had to force a tube with a light on the end down into my lungs to look around. It hurt terribly. He discovered mucous plugs, and the very thing the doctors had feared, pneumonia. Back on the respirator I went, and the hated ET tube was forced down my nose and throat again. My doctor didn't think I should go through another surgery, so he recommended that I not have another trach.

Every few hours, a respiratory therapist suctioned my lungs and did chest percussion. That hurt, too. Everything hurt, it seemed. Another tube was inserted in my other nostril to feed me. The only good thing about that tube was that I didn't have to taste the medicine; they poured that down the tube, too.

My nurses fed me a high-protein liquid diet. Every four hours, I felt a cold liquid slide down my throat through the tube. What a weird feeling it was to want to swallow but not need to.

For the next five days, I was on the respirator and fed through the tube. Finally, I passed the crisis, and began breathing easier. The hated tube was pulled out of my nose and I breathed alone again.

My doctor had to look around in my lungs again, so I had another bronchoscopy. The pain was sharp.

All the ups and downs of my condition were really harder to take than if I had stayed one way or the other. It seemed I was always either in an encouraging upswing or disheartening decline.

By this time, I weighed only 87 pounds and looked like a victim of anorexia nervosa. I had no padding at all on my 5′ 5″ frame, and every touch, even in love, hurt. Heavily medicated, I was drowsy and groggy much of the time while I was on the respirator.

It seemed like no one could understand what I needed. I became very frustrated when I had to mouth something over and over. I felt hot all the time, and when the nurses gave me ice chips, foam bubbled out of my nose.

By Saturday, a week after I first was put on the respirator, I had recovered enough to have the NG tube removed and eat alone. On Sunday, Tom arrived to find his wife eating a tuna fish sandwich and looking somewhat human again.

It was good to be off the machines. Within a few days I was in better spirits and telling my doctors that I would walk someday.

Jeffrey was my little joy. He grew and thrived and was able to leave the hospital shortly after I was disconnected from the respirator. I felt badly that I hadn't been able to care for him while in the hospital, and that he wasn't able to go home to his mommy and daddy.

I knew that Jeffrey would be in good hands until I got better, though. Russ and Janis had two youngsters, and they had offered before Jeff's birth to care for him until we could do it. They lived only a mile from us, and we were delighted to accept their offer.

Big-hearted Janis had her hands full with little Jeffrey. Hungry as a baby bird, he had to be fed every few hours. Because he was so weak, he wanted to eat but couldn't swallow very well so he had to be force-fed at first.

Tom went over to visit his tiny son nearly every day, and Janis would often feed both my husband and my son. I wanted so badly to be making dinner for them, but since that was impossible, I was thankful to Janis for her help.

11

B Y THE END OF FEBRUARY, I had improved a little. I was eating well, feeling stronger—and determined to walk again. About this time, I received a letter from a grade-school girlfriend, Ann Ernst, who worked in Washington, D.C. She wondered if I had heard anything about an experimental treatment which was being tested on GBS victims at Johns Hopkins Hospital in Baltimore, Maryland. One of Ann's friends had contracted GBS several years earlier and had looked into the program, called plasma exchange. He didn't undergo the treatments, but he gave Ann several pamphlets explaining it.

I asked a doctor about the treatments, but he said it was normally used to treat other diseases, and it was too early to really tell if it was effective for GBS-like diseases. I let the matter drop, since he offered no encouragement. Besides, I was still expecting instant healing soon.

Because I was back on a high dosage of steroids again, the moon face, insatiable appetite, insomnia, and bloated stomach returned. Then the severe headaches started. Up and down, up and down, went my health, as if I were on some sort of seesaw.

I was trying to apply St. Paul's words to my situation, "I have learned, in whatsoever state I am, therewith to be content" (Phil. 4:12), but I wasn't doing a very good job of it. I was much more content when I was feeling good than when I was sick.

As before, strength slowly returned as my body fought the disease, and by March 3 I was able to return home. I was still quadriplegic, but stable and out of danger.

I was grateful to the doctors and nurses for all their help. Their good care helped both Jeffrey and I survive.

Years before, I had dreamed of someday walking out of a hospital with my husband beside me and a little blue-blanketed bundle of joy in my arms. Reality included a wheelchair, hospital bed, nursing care for me . . . and no baby. Although Russ and Janis often brought Jeffrey to visit us, I still felt his absence sharply. Because they cared for Jeff as though he were their own, though, the separation was bearable.

We hired Mary Ellen, Evelyn, Tina, and Deb to care for me again when I returned home. They had stuck by me through a lot of turmoil, and were willing to care for me again. We knew it wasn't for the money; they could have made much more working elsewhere and with easier work. No amount of money could have paid for the kind of loving care they gave me.

I hadn't slept in a regular bed for a year and a half. Often in the middle of the night I longed to hear Tom breathing beside me, but he wasn't there. Now that I was home again, I decided to sleep in our bed. *Surely I'll be able to sleep well at last, safe in my own bed,* I thought.

Wrong. I was still in too much pain, and beds were terribly uncomfortable. I was used to hospital beds that could be raised or lowered to make me more comfortable.

All through the night, I wanted daylight to come so I could get up. Because I couldn't sleep, neither could Tom. It was a long, uncomfortable night—far different than the relaxing, peaceful night I had hoped for. Every nerve in my body seemed on fire.

The next morning I decided that I would have to go back to the hospital bed, for Tom's sake as much as mine. He had to get some sleep because he worked every day. I needed sleep so that I wouldn't get weaker again.

Tom called my doctor, who suggested I take more pain medication before going to bed to help me sleep through the night. Despite the medication, I kept waking up, and my prayers didn't take the pain away.

Angry at myself because I couldn't take the pain, I called to Tom to help me. The bedroom is in the back of the house, and at first he didn't hear me.

"Tom. Help me!" I yelled.

Finally he stumbled out, half asleep. He gave me pain medication and fixed me a snack. I was ravenous all the time from the medicine I was on, although I didn't gain weight.

I felt terrible for waking him up, but I just couldn't stand the pain anymore. If I could have moved to help myself, I would have. I tried ignoring the pain, but I couldn't.

Still half asleep, Tom mumbled a good-night and went back to bed. *I'll bet he's sorry he's stuck with me,* I thought.

The next morning, Tom left for work at six, looking exhausted. He gave me a quick good-bye kiss before he left.

"You'll be OK until Evelyn gets here?" he asked.

"I should be fine. I'll just sleep," I told him.

My nurse would arrive about 9 a.m. and stay until Tom got home. We wanted to try getting along with only part-time nursing care, if we could.

I fell asleep again after Tom left, still in some pain, but not as much as during the night. A short time later, I was awakened by a fly perched on my nose.

"Get off," I told it, wrinkling my nostrils, then blowing through them. The fly crawled leisurely onto my cheek, where it was joined by a comrade. Their explorations tickled my face and made it impossible to relax.

I screwed my face up, twitching my muscles and wiggling my

tongue. Far from being frightened away, the flies seemed to enjoy the ride. Finally they flew off, but they returned periodically to torment me.

I was relieved when Evelyn arrived so she could brush the flies from my face. They were driving me crazy by that time.

The next morning, before Tom left for work, he pulled the sheet over my head. Even though we couldn't always keep flies out of the house, no matter how careful we were, we foiled them with the sheet trick.

I looked forward to Jeffrey's daily visits. I longed to hug and kiss him and change his diapers. Instead, I had to be content to watch him, and to hold him with Janis' help. She kept me filled in on all the cute things he did.

He changed so much so fast. I was amazed at his strength and alertness. Jeffrey seemed to notice everything.

"He's a bright little boy, Carol," Janis said.

I agreed. With his dark hair and eyes, he was an exceptionally cute baby.

"Jeffrey. Hi, baby, I'm your mommy, I love you," I would whisper softly as someone held him on my lap. It bothered me that my son might not know who I was. I wanted my baby at home, but it was impossible. He needed constant care and I needed constant care. There was no way Tom could cope with all that, even with help. I didn't want him to try until Jeff was a little bigger or I was a little better.

Jeff needed to know who his mommy and daddy were. I knew that, and I was determined to get well enough to take care of him at home.

He doesn't know that I'm his mommy. He doesn't want me, I would think sometimes when he would squirm and cry while lying on my stomach. "Lord, please let Jeff know me and love me," I prayed many times.

I received a letter from Linda Bemis, who had been one of my home nurses earlier. Enclosed were some clippings on plasma exchange, the same treatment my friend Ann had written to me about. According to the clippings, plasma exchange, known as P.E., was being tried on an experimental basis in a few major research hospitals, and the results appeared to be positive.

I hadn't really forgotten about the plasma exchange, but Linda's letter prompted me to action. My sister Judy put together my medical history, sent it to Johns Hopkins, and asked them to send us information on the program. I was feeling stronger again, but I wanted to explore every possible method of being healed. If this plasma exchange was something that could cure me, I wanted to know about it. I firmly believe that the Lord heals through doctors and has given human beings the knowledge and technology to perform miracles.

By mid-April, though, I was so much better that my doctors discontinued my medication. I was able to sit up in my wheelchair for ten hours, and I was showing improvements every day. We received the information on plasma exchange, but didn't pursue it because things were going so well.

By early May, Jeffrey was sleeping through the night. Russ and Janis were willing to keep him longer, but Tom and I were eager to have him come home as soon as possible.

What a joy it was to have our three-month-old son living with us at last. We were finally a real family. The tranquility didn't last long, though. Beginning the first night Jeffrey was at home, he would wake up several times during the night, crying. Tom would get up, give Jeff a bottle and try to comfort him. Tom and I were both exhausted; we hadn't planned on being up all night with our little boy. We couldn't understand why Jeff was waking up, because he had been sleeping through the night at the Watsons.

Theo, a good friend who had helped care for me, said, "Carol, if you continue to let Jeff get used to getting up during the night and being fed, you'll still be getting up with him when he's a year old. Maybe you'll just have to let him cry."

The next night, we decided to let him cry. It was terrible. He screamed at the top of his lungs for nearly an hour. I felt guilty to be a mother who couldn't even get up and comfort her baby. If I could have moved, I know I would have gone to him, regardless of what we had decided was best. It's a horrible feeling to hear your baby cry and not be able to go to him.

Luckily, Tom had more sense and stuck by our original agreement. Neither of us got much sleep. Tom's room was right next to Jeff's, and he could hear Jeff's wails. He got up to check on him a few times. Once I heard the door slam when he went back to bed, and I knew it was getting to him. Tom showed frustration so seldom that I knew he must be pretty upset.

"Oh, Lord, this doesn't seem like the way it should be. I'm finally home, Jeff is finally home, but we don't seem like the happy family I imagined. Help us, please," I prayed.

One night was all it took. The next night, our boy slept through until morning without waking up at all. Our baby was home to stay.

My nurses and our friends and neighbors continued to help us. They dressed Jeffrey and diapered and rocked him during the day. He received a lot of love, which I knew was important for his emotional health. Without their compassion and love, I don't know if Jeff would have continued to grow and thrive as well as he did.

Every day, someone would lay Jeff on the hospital bed beside me. I couldn't actually hold him or play with him, but I could talk with him and sing to him.

Toward the end of May, I had gotten strong enough to feed myself. I was pretty sloppy, but at least I was hitting my mouth fairly often.

"Look, I'm eating with a spoon before Jeffrey learned to do it," I laughed one day. "I'll walk before he does, too."

"With the Lord's help, I'm going to be able to walk and cook and care for my family," I often told myself.

Best of all, I grew strong enough to hold Jeff's bottle. Someone else had to burp him, but I was finally feeding him.

Little things became possible again. For the first time in 2½ years, I was able to hold silverware and brush my teeth. This was all so exciting for me, especially because the doctors were afraid my body had been permanently damaged and would never regain mobility.

Day by day I could move my arms and legs more, until one day early in June, with the help of my home physical therapist, I walked a bit on crutches. I was pretty awkward, but I could move around the house for a few minutes before I had to sit down again. After being in a sitting or lying-down position for so long, I felt that I was mastering quite a skill.

"I *will* walk before Jeff does, Tom, I *will*," I told him. "The Lord is working a miracle right now!"

"You're doing great," he encouraged me.

I started writing a little. My handwriting was sloppy, but legible. I wrote notes to thank people for their help and let them know how I was doing.

The more independent I became, the happier I felt. I was able to lift 4 or 5 pounds per arm and 8 pounds per leg in therapy— more weight than I had lifted in three years.

One morning I managed to struggle into some clothes by myself. After that I dressed myself as often as possible. I would wheel myself into the kitchen and cook breakfast. The first meal I had cooked in $2\frac{1}{2}$ years was eggs and toast.

I wheeled the chair over to the stove, locked it, and stood at the stove until I tired, which was usually within a few minutes. Cooking anything took quite awhile, but it was worth the effort.

All my life I had enjoyed domestic things like baking, cooking, and sewing, so being back in my kitchen again was a joy. I even began making Jeff's formula, and I popped popcorn for Tom.

Bob and Charlene invited us to their church, and we really enjoyed it. The nondenominational church stressed learning the Scriptures thoroughly, and I drank it all in. I felt as though I had been thirsty for so long, but never paid much attention to what I was really thirsty for. Now I knew. I couldn't get enough of learning about the Bible.

When we went to church, I walked on my crutches, and someone was beside me to balance me. It was so good to be able to go to church again.

Life was good, and kept getting better.

"Tom, let's take a step of faith and send back the hospital bed and the lift. We won't need it," I exuberantly told my husband after an especially good day.

"Sounds good," he agreed.

I was delighted to send the equipment back to the rental company. Our living room finally looked like a real living room again. The bed and lift had taken up most of the space during the past 20 months.

I found out later that even though my case was unusually severe, and one of my doctors said he had never seen one as bad, I had also been protected from the countless complications that can set in. Many people in hospitals die of complications, but, as my doctor noted in his report, "Outside of the muscular and sensory failure, the patient had a remarkably smooth hospital course without the plethora of complications which can accompany a chronic debilitated patient of this nature."

The Lord had protected me. I could so easily have died or suffered permanent damage. Now that we knew my body was healing, the big question was whether another relapse would hit me. I was positive that I was well, and that the Lord was healing me. I could even begin to see a lot of good that had come out of my long struggle to recover.

"Carol, see? We knew all along the Lord would heal you. Praise him!" Charlene told me.

I was praising him and thanking him. My faith seemed to grow stronger along with my body.

Jeffrey was 5½ months old in mid-July, when I noticed the all-too-familiar tingling and numbness in my fingers again.

"Oh, Lord, please protect me. I'm doing so well," I begged.

Yet Tom and I could do nothing but watch helplessly as all the progress I had made slowly disintegrated. I noted the disappointment in Tom's face in unguarded moments, and I wondered how much more he could take.

12

Back came my long-time companions, the hospital bed and hydraulic lift. This time we put them in the back bedroom, trusting that I wouldn't need them much longer.

I was bewildered. But I was not about to give up. Charlene and Bob were puzzled, too, I found later. They continued to encourage me, though.

I have been through so much trauma. Near-death, childbirth, isolation, loneliness, humiliation, depression, I thought. *The Lord brought me safely through it all so far. I'm not going to stop trusting him now.*

Despite my prayers, the relapse continued relentlessly, and I grew helpless again. We just kept praying for a miracle. Hebrews 11:1 says, "Faith is the substance of things hoped for, the evidence of things not seen." Charlene, Bob, Tom, and my family and friends decided to stand fast, believing that I would walk again.

I believe there is a reason for everything. I couldn't help crying some and feeling sad to see my hard-earned progress slip away, yet I knew that God was in control of the situation. Maybe

I wasn't ever going to receive an instant healing, but I still felt certain I would walk again.

I couldn't get the plasma exchange experimental program out of my mind. I began to feel that God had guided Ann and Linda to send me the information. As I reread the clippings, I grew more and more excited. Although there were no guarantees, some GBS victims were showing promising results.

I decided that since the program was experimental, I could be healed at the same time I helped other victims by being part of the program. Maybe that was why I was led to this point. I didn't know. Who can know how the Lord works? I did know that I wanted to try to get into the program.

"Lord, please guide us. Get me into that program if it's your will," I prayed.

Tom was a little less enthusiastic. He had seen my hopes dashed so often, and he knew that Johns Hopkins was a 10-hour trip. Not only would the trip be hard on me, it would mean more separation from him and Jeff.

"Tom, we've at least got to try to get into the program. If this is what our lives would be like, relapse after relapse, it will be hard on both of us. I think God is leading us to this," I insisted.

So we called Johns Hopkins and talked to one of the doctors, a specialist familiar with the plasma exchange program. After going over my medical records and discussing my history, he said they would examine me if I came to Baltimore.

"There are no guarantees that we'll put you in the program. But we will examine you," he said.

I was excited after we hung up. I knew this meant more hospitals and separation from my family, but I was willing to try it.

Experimental. The word didn't bother me anymore. I knew I would be a bit of a guinea pig, but I was ready for it. Now if they would just let me into the program. That became our prayer.

Preparation for our trip was quickly done. Tom had outfitted our van with a bed for carting me back and forth to the hospital, so we planned to drive it to Baltimore.

Several friends and Tom's mom offered to watch Jeffrey for us. I knew I would miss him terribly, but we couldn't take him along.

Tom carried me out to the van. My sister Judy had rearranged her schedule to go with us, and soon we were off to Baltimore. Tom and Judy took turns driving, and after a rainy night on the road we arrived early Sunday morning. I missed Jeffrey already, and was beginning to feel sorry for myself at being so helpless again.

"Lord, help me not to be discouraged," I prayed. "Thank you for your work in whatever our situation."

I was admitted that day, August 3, nearly helpless again. I could roll over and that was about it.

"We'll have to keep you awhile for tests and observation. Then, if it seems that the program may help, you'll be here for a few weeks," my doctor said. I was a little awed to be at such a famous hospital.

I looked at Tom and realized how much I hated to leave him again. Yet I believed that the Lord had led me here. Still, I felt sad when he had to say good-bye and leave.

I learned that plasma exchange has been used to treat other diseases for about 20 years, but only a few hospitals in the country were trying it on victims of GBS and similar diseases.

After several days of tests, I grew weaker still. I was in a lot of pain, and I cried. My nurses were patient and understanding.

"Carol, we're going to start you on the treatments. There are no guarantees, but we'll give it a try," the doctor who was in charge of giving me the treatments, told me after the tests were completed. A total of three specialists, one of them a neurologist, were working with me.

"Thank you, Lord!" I was so excited I couldn't stop smiling.

"Hi, Carol, how are you today?" asked a girl who introduced herself as Terry. She and Katie were the nurses who hooked me up to a machine and gave me the treatments.

Basically, plasma exchange is a process that drains your blood and exchanges the old plasma for fresh plasma. The theory is that something in the plasma is causing the disease, and by replacing it regularly, the disease can be controlled and possibly eventually eliminated.

The machine was large but on wheels, and it was brought into my room to my bedside. My doctor, Terry, and Katie were gentle, but since my veins were so small and weak, they had to use femoral catheters, which were large needles inserted into the femoral vein in the groin area. This was extremely painful, and they had to numb the area before they could insert the catheter.

The first time they inserted the catheter, I was afraid I would pass out. The room began to spin and I felt queasy. Then I got hold of myself, and everything went well. I had been poked and prodded so often in the past three years that I was used to pain. This wasn't too bad.

The machine took two liters of my plasma, which was spun off from the rest of my blood in a centrifuge and discarded. My white blood cells, red blood cells, and platelets were returned to my body.

I had seven treatments during the four-week stay. After four treatments, I began getting stronger. It was working! Tom and Judy were as excited as I was when I phoned them.

"Carol, we've diagnosed a slightly different form of your condition," my doctor told me one day.

"What's the difference?" I asked him.

"Your condition is relapsing. There is always the danger of it returning once you have worked your way to health, as you found out. We call it chronic, relapsing inflammatory polyradiculoneuropathy, a much more rare and more serious condition than acute GBS. With plasma exchange, we take out the probable culprit, your plasma, and exchange it for healthy plasma, so there's hope of recovery."

I was still confused. Still another diagnosis! However, I felt confident that I was in the right place, and at last had been led

135

to a cure for my baffling disease. If anyone could help me, these doctors could.

———◆———

Because I was so far from home, I didn't get many visitors. My nurses, especially Kathy and Ivana, treated me with respect and kindness, treatment that made a world of difference in how I felt.

The Lord provided the comfort of friends, even so far from home. One day Dave and Sharon Rex walked into my room.

"What in the world are you doing here?" I gasped in surprise. I still thought of Dave as my boss, even though I hadn't taught in nearly three years.

"Hi," he smiled. "We were on our way to visit my brother in New Jersey and decided to make a little detour."

Throughout my illness, wherever I was, the Rexes came to visit me. I thanked them for their care and concern.

Another day, my friend Jean, who had been my occupational therapist at the rehab center in Ohio, walked into my room to surprise me. She had moved to Baltimore, and was working at Johns Hopkins.

Another familiar face was Ann, my girlhood friend who had told me of plasma exchange in the first place. She lived nearby, and came to visit several times a week.

"You can go home in a few days," the doctor told me near the end of August.

"Really! Great!" I couldn't wait to see Tom and Jeff again. I had been gone four long weeks.

Tom was excited by my progress. It had been so long since I had been on my feet, and now I was walking two or three steps, with the help of crutches and other people. My nerves and muscles were making another comeback.

After the long trip home, I couldn't wait to see Jeffrey. I could actually hug him again. He squirmed and bounced, but seemed happy to see me, too.

For 10 days I improved. Once again I was dressing, bathing, eating alone, and standing. Then I grew weaker again.

We called my doctor and told him I was getting worse again. Two weeks later, I was readmitted to Johns Hopkins.

"Another autumn, another hospital," I thought as I waited in my room for a treatment. A twinge of sadness came over me as I thought of my kids and home economics room and football games. But that was another life, long ago.

I felt optimistic about the plasma exchange, and was eager to begin again. Some of the doctors were skeptical about how much good they would do, but I begged them to continue treatments.

"Oh, God, I can't believe you would let me get this far for nothing," I cried.

The doctors decided to continue treatments; perhaps I was an especially stubborn case. My veins were so damaged from being attached to machines that my doctors decided to create an artificial vein for future treatments. Called a bovine (or AV) shunt, this vein was surgically placed in my right arm. Until the shunt healed in about six weeks, they planned to use the femoral vein. No one knew how many treatments I would need to have.

My new friend Lloyd was a real encouragement to me. He suffered from the same disease I had. Tall, white-haired Lloyd came to visit me every Sunday. He realized that I was far from family and home, and he knew how lonely a hospital can be.

I wanted my doctors to put me on the same medication that Lloyd was taking. I saw him improve, and I knew they could do the same for me.

By the end of October, after eight treatments, I was ready to be dismissed again. I was much stronger, and I kept improving for another 10 days after I returned home. Jeff loved grabbing at my crutches as I moved around the house. Sometimes his scooter and my crutches collided.

My doctors had anticipated another decline, and when it came, they made arrangements to have me admitted to the University of Michigan Hospital in Ann Arbor, which was only 90 miles from home. The U. of M. had facilities for plasma exchange, but hadn't used it on my form of disease before.

Dr. Albers and Dr. McLean, neurologists at the U. of M., agreed to take my case. So when the decline started, Tom and I packed things up again and headed to Ann Arbor.

The November wind cut through me as Tom helped me into a wheelchair. Another new hospital meant learning our way around again, but we were used to that by now. We were grateful to have been admitted to a hospital so close to home.

Nearly paralyzed again, I was given a treatment the day after I arrived. The shunt in my arm was used for the first time, and it worked just fine. Instead of getting only a two-liter exchange, I was able to have a four-liter exchange.

Unfortunately, due to my medication, my white blood count dropped dangerously low, and I was put into isolation. I was in isolation for a week before my count rose enough to fight off infections.

Tom came to visit me while I was in isolation. He had to wear a mask and gown to protect me from "bugs."

"You look like a robber," I teased him, "or a doctor."

Tom was doing well. He looked pretty tired most of the time, but he seemed in good spirits.

After leaving isolation, I returned to my room and my PE treatments, which were every several days. One day my doctor asked me to answer questions at a "grand round" session. I was wheeled into a big room full of doctors, and my doctor briefly explained my history. He checked my reflexes and grip in front of all the doctors; at the time I was so weak that I had no grip or strength in my hands or legs.

"How well do you expect to get, Carol?" asked one of the doctors.

I immediately assured him, "I may not run and I may not play softball again, but I do plan to be basically normal. With God's help, I plan to be able to take care of my husband and son and house."

After the meeting, one of the doctors came into my room.

"Carol," he began, "when are you going to start being realistic?"

I was so hurt and upset that I couldn't answer at first. I felt that we were close to the answer through PE. I didn't want them to stop, not when we were so close. I knew they were thinking of discontinuing the treatments and putting me back on steroids, the same treatment I had been on over the past years.

"What do you mean? How can you think I'm not realistic?" I asked him. "I have a wheelchair at home, a hospital bed, and a lift. That's real, I know it's there, and I'm not giving them away. I just feel that I am getting better, and I don't want you to take away my hope of a good recovery."

When he left the room, I cried. It just seemed that everywhere I went for medical help, I had encountered so much doubt and opposition, and so little encouragement that I would completely recover.

This time, I wasn't giving in without a fight, though. I believed strongly that the Lord had led me to PE.

"Tom, Jeff, and I need to be a family. I need to do my share and not just sit on the sidelines. I want to help care for my baby!" I thought. "We are so close to having our prayers answered!"

In all fairness, I could understand why the doctors felt I was being unreasonable. My history didn't look good. In fact, it looked pretty bleak.

I stayed in the hospital until the middle of December, receiving plasma exchange several times a week. The doctors and nurses were amazed and delighted at my progress.

I made a wooden duck pull-toy for Jeff in occupational therapy. I also baked cupcakes and made a pizza, which I shared with the nurses. My physical therapist, Barb, patiently worked with me until I was able to use Canadian crutches, which attach at the elbow. Because of the shunt in my arm, I couldn't use regular crutches.

Barb helped me take brief, halting walks around the therapy

room with the crutches. As I looked around at all the other injured and paralyzed people, some with trachs, I thought about what I had been through and how the Lord had brought me such a long way. I just hoped that these people would continue their fight for health and not give up.

When Tom came to take me home, he was happy to see my progress. When I had been admitted five weeks earlier, I couldn't dress, feed myself, or rise from my wheelchair. Now I was doing all that, plus more. I could even blow-dry my hair! We were in high spirits as we drove home.

13

THE DAY I ARRIVED HOME, I cooked supper for us from my wheelchair. I had been able to get around the hospital on my crutches and stand for longer periods than I had in four years. But I didn't want to have to worry about Jeffrey, now 10½ months old, and his little scooter getting entangled in my crutches again like they had the last time I was home. He had thought they were a great game, and would race around on his scooter, right at my feet.

"No, no, honey, let mommy's crutches alone," I would say.

Jeffrey would chuckle his deep baby chuckle and hang onto my crutches. I was afraid I would lose my balance and fall on him, so it was tough to get around.

I didn't want my crutches in the way this time, so I took a deep breath, told Tom, "OK, I said I would walk alone before Jeff did, and so here goes."

I stood up from my wheelchair, balanced against the sink, and walked a few steps to the refrigerator. Supporting myself against the wall, I walked toward the living room, let go of the wall, and took a step. Then I took another, and another. Slowly, awkwardly, but by myself, I walked across the room to Tom. *I walked across my living room alone. I walked before my son did, and I didn't stumble or fall.*

"Tom! I did it! I walked alone!" I was laughing with excitement.

He hugged me close. For a minute I thought I might see my husband cry again, but this time for a very different reason.

"Oh, Lord, thank you. Thank you." I felt such happiness, and I remembered a very special Scripture: "They that wait upon the Lord shall renew their strength; they shall mount up with wings as eagles; they shall run, and not be weary; and they shall walk, and not faint" (Isa. 40:31).

I had waited a long time, longer than I had expected to. But despite all the odds against me and the fact that nearly every doctor had told me to stop planning to walk again, *I was walking.* Step by step, day by day, God had been with me. Best of all, along the journey, rough as it was, I had come to know Jesus as my Lord and Savior.

———————◆———————

My sister Diane invited us to her wedding in Fort Loramie, the little Ohio town in which I grew up. It was a cold and snowy day, and I used my crutches to walk into the church, with Tom holding tightly to my arm.

As we walked down the aisle to our seats, Dad, my sisters and brothers, our friends and relatives, watched us with joy in their faces. A lot of people knew I was back at home, but had no idea how strong I was. I saw tears in many eyes, and I had to cry, too.

"Carol, this is the best wedding present you could have given Steve and me," Diane smiled after the ceremony. Her wedding was the first family celebration I had been able to participate in for a long time. I felt kind of silly in my tennis shoes when everyone else was all dressed up, but it was the only way I could walk.

A few days later, I received the best Christmas present of my life. I was able to change Jeff's diaper all by myself. That might not be a thrilling event to some folks, but Dec. 24 will always be an occasion to celebrate the first time I could really care for my baby in a practical way. It was a bit awkward, true, with Jeff in his playpen and me sitting in the wheelchair, but we were able to adapt to the situation.

Our house was gaily decorated for our first Christmas as a family. The tree and ornaments were fascinating to Jeffrey, and the next time I changed his diaper I found evidence that he had developed a taste for tinsel. We tried to barricade the tree after that.

Tom's mom and dad invited us to their home for Christmas dinner, and it was such a treat to be able to walk around like everyone else, laughing and singing. In the house, I didn't need crutches at all anymore.

I dressed our little boy on Christmas Day. For so many months I had dreamed of doing this. Jeffrey looked adorable in his new Christmas outfit. I looked at him, racing around in his little scooter, and thanked the Lord for our miracle baby.

After Christmas, I progressed from cooking from the wheelchair to leaning against the stove to standing alone. I still tired easily, and sometimes I needed to rely on the chair or crutches. I started sewing with a needle and thread. Hemlines had changed in the years that I had been wearing mostly hospital gowns, and I hemmed my clothing to a more stylish length.

Dishes can be a drudgery, but for me they were therapy. Washing dishes strengthened my hands, so I could rejoice, even in doing the dishes.

A week after Christmas, I took a tub bath by myself—my first in more than three years. I had to crawl in and out of the tub, but it was such a luxury to sit and soak in all that hot water.

The day after my bath, I started getting numbness and tingling again. The PE treatment was wearing off. I grew weaker over the next few days, so I called my doctor. He wasn't too worried, because they knew a decline was probable. We all realized by

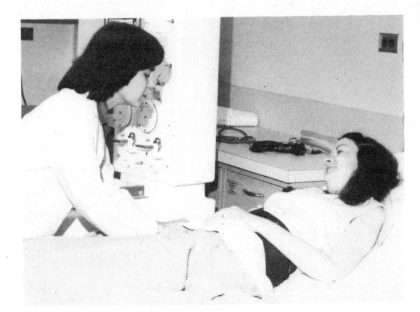

Plasma exchange treatments take several hours. The doctors, nurses, and technicians are gentle and patient.

Tom and Jeffrey are my gifts from God. Jeffrey, at 2½, is a healthy, talkative little boy.

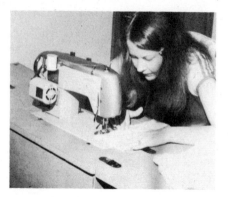

It was wonderful to be able to sew again. My first project was a little blue playsuit for Jeffrey.

Bob and Charlene Lantz, my dear friends, gave me this rug to hook when I was a quadriplegic.

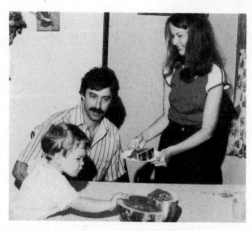

Watermelon has always been a favorite fruit of Tom's, and Jeffrey and I love it too.

now that my body just needed time to heal, and the treatments were working.

Tom drove me back to Ann Arbor and readmitted me to the hospital. I only had to stay for nine days. While I was there, I received three treatments and spent a lot of time visiting with other patients. I tried to cheer them up. So many people had cheered me up when I was down that I wanted to pass on the love. Sometimes I just wheeled around and introduced myself to people to get to know them. Many people were afraid of what might happen to them, and I could understand how they felt.

My doctors decided that I would continue under their care, but as an outpatient. Together we would work toward regulating treatments and medication until my body was completely healed. They still didn't make any promises, but I could see how well my body was responding.

Early in February, I was doing so well that Tom and I decided we wouldn't need any outside help. Both paid and volunteer persons had assisted us for more than three years. Without these unselfish women, who were cheerful and pleasant even when I was not, our ordeal might have been too much for us. They truly let the love of Christ shine through their lives.

I began driving again. Nearly four years earlier, just before Tom and I were married, I had renewed my driver's license. The Lord's timing is perfect. He got me back driving again just in time to renew my license before it expired. I really didn't want to have to take a test again and prove I could parallel park. That was tough enough the first time!

I began carrying Jeff alone that spring. He weighed 26 pounds and was strong and feisty. My doctors now declared me "80% normal," much to their surprise.

When word got around the community that I was back on my feet, church groups began asking me to come and tell them about my experiences and how the Lord helped us through. I was pretty nervous the first time, but was happy to be able to share how good God is.

Early in June of 1981, my doctor made an appointment for me to have another artificial vein—a shunt—put in my arm. The first shunt had already clotted off, and my veins were still too weak to use. I had too much scar tissue in my groin area to have more femoral sticks, so a new shunt was our only safe choice. I dreaded still another operation.

When I went in for the operation, it was delayed. The doctors decided to wait a few days. I was a little frustrated, because it was a two-hour drive to Ann Arbor, but I figured it would all work out.

Physically I was feeling good. The treatments were allowing me to live a nearly normal life with Tom and Jeff. I walked with only a limp, and I could cook, clean, and sew. I knew I needed to go in for a treatment whenever the tingling began, though; that was my warning. As long as I continued my steroid medication and had a treatment before I grew too weak, I was all right and fought off the declines.

My sister Pat and I drove up to Ann Arbor for the operation a few days later. We stopped at a restaurant for lunch, and I heard someone yell "Carol!" Vicki Hesterman came hurrying across the room to greet me. I couldn't believe that we were both eating at the same place at the same time in Michigan; she lived in California and I lived in Ohio.

Vicki was surprised to see me. We had talked briefly about doing a book some time earlier, but were both too busy to do much about it. I had taught school with her mother, Phyllis, an art teacher, and had met Vicki six years ago at a dinner in their home. Phyllis had told Vicki about my illness, and kept her up-to-date on my progress.

"This is amazing," she said. "I was just telling my friend about a writing project I am working on in Michigan, and you walked in the door."

We decided that maybe it was the right time to seriously con-

147

sider doing a book about my experiences. That chance encounter in Ann Arbor was the catalyst.

We enjoyed a good meal with Vicki and her friend, and I filled them in with the details of my progress. We made plans to work on an outline before she returned to California.

After lunch Pat dropped me off at the hospital, and things seemed to go wrong again. I waited an hour, expecting to be admitted for a several-day stay, when one of my doctors came in.

"Go home, Carol. Something came up and we can't do your surgery. I'll call you in a week or so and we'll reschedule it," he said. I knew this might happen; they were trying to squeeze me into an already tight schedule.

I was getting a little anxious. It took awhile for these shunts to heal; what if I needed another plasma exchange before mine healed?

I had no choice but to call home for someone to pick me up. At least I hadn't unpacked yet.

My doctor didn't call that week, and by the time I went back to the hospital, needing another PE and wondering where they would be able to stick a needle, my doctor had good news for me.

"Carol, it looks like you won't need that shunt after all," he said with a smile.

"Why?" I asked, expecting another delay.

"Your veins have healed enough so that we can use them," he told me.

Only God could heal veins that quickly, especially veins as damaged as mine had been. Several people were praying with me that I wouldn't need the operation, and I didn't. My body was definitely healing.

My relapses were coming less frequently now, generally about every two to three weeks. At last, we apparently had them under control. Charlene and Bob, still our dear friends, were thrilled that our prayers were being answered. We enjoyed attending their church, and did so regularly.

Tom took me to Toledo for our fourth wedding anniversary

on June 18. We ate dinner in a nice restaurant, and I thought to myself, *This is a lot different than the last time Tom took me to Toledo, in a wheelchair.*

We had a fun, romantic evening. I smiled at him across the table and told him, "I love you so much." I couldn't have told him how much.

In August, we went to visit my dad's farm for the first time in more than four years.

"Jeff, this is where I grew up. I milked the cows and helped bale hay here," I told my little boy as I showed him the farm. He was too small to understand, but he seemed to enjoy himself immensely, running all over the barnyard. At a year and a half, Jeffrey's energy was boundless.

My dad was excited to have his little grandson visit him. We all spent the night and drove home the next day.

A week later, I stepped on a toy while I was carrying Jeff.

"Oh, Lord, help," I thought as I headed toward the floor.

I hit the floor hard, but thank God, Jeff wasn't hurt. He landed on me. I lay there for about 15 minutes. The pain was excruciating, as my body was still very tender and sensitive to bumps and blows. Finally, I felt strong enough to crawl over to the couch.

Jeff seemed to be enjoying the whole event. He thought it was great that his mommy was down on the floor playing with him, and he bounced up and down on me.

Although I was getting along well at home, and taking good care of Jeff, little falls or accidents were still more crucial for us than for most families.

In early September, Jeff jumped off the bed and sprained his leg and ankle. He couldn't walk on it for a week, and since he is extremely active, it was hard to keep him quiet.

"Come on, honey, play with mommy. Let's read a book," I would say as I entertained Jeff until Tom came home.

The leaves began falling from the trees in our yard in October. At last I wasn't in a hospital room during autumn.

I put Jeff's sweatshirt on him, found our rake, and began

raking the leaves in huge piles. Jeff had loads of fun jumping in my big piles, and as fast as I got a pile together, my mischievous little boy scattered them. Tom came home and helped us, and the two of us were able to outrake Jeff's scattering.

Christmas of 1981 was the first time my whole family had been together in five years. We celebrated at my dad's farm. I was walking and eating, Jeffrey was getting into everything, and my sisters and I were talking so much that Dad, Tom, and my brothers could hardly get in a word.

In April 1982, I "ran" down our lane for the first time in five years. I was awkward, and would certainly win no races, but I *ran,* with a slow, lurching gait. Again, the psalm ran through my mind, "they shall run, and not be weary. . . ." Not only could I walk, against all the odds, I could *run!*

14

MY SISTER JUDY RECENTLY WROTE ME a letter and asked if I remembered the time she came to visit me in the hospital when I nearly died in the fall of 1978:

Dear Carol, Thanks for your lovely letter. I have been thinking about you a lot lately. I remember when you were in Intensive Care, rushed in from the rehab center that night. We thought you had a heart attack, and there were other complications rumored. All the family rushed to the hospital to see you —honestly wondering if it would be the last time. Les and I went up with some others of the family. The nurse got very upset with us as we were trying to be by your bedside, someone at all times. I couldn't believe how different you looked than the last time I had seen you, sitting on the lawn in your wheelchair. You had the same head and face although tubes were coming out everywhere, but I was aghast to believe that that was all there was of your body. And then we were told that you only weighed 87 pounds. Not being a Christian at the time, I prayed that God would take you. I couldn't stand the pain of seeing you suffer.

Even back then, I knew that God would have his way, and if you pulled through, it was because of something more than the doctors could do. In my heart, I felt terribly guilty for praying for you to die. Was I trying to make it easier on us? I don't know. I knew I loved you and always would. Even though Mother had died, we didn't have to watch it.

When we came back to see you, I noticed there were bubbles around the large tube in your nose. I tried to wipe them off with a tissue. I wasn't even sure you knew I was there. Then a nurse came in with a suction machine which did a much better job of getting rid of the bubbles.

Tom was his usual self, composed but very inward. He took the stress better than anyone I've ever seen. I remember his being out in the lounge with Les. At the time, I didn't understand how he could do it. He had already stayed at the hospital a full week, sleeping in the lounges in his regular clothes. Where does this kind of love come from?

All our love in Him,
Judy and girls.

I thank God for Tom. And I, too, often wondered where his love came from. Whenever I asked him why he stuck things out, he wouldn't say much. When we were working on this book, Vicki talked with Tom privately about what made him stay with me when so many couples, even Christians, divorce for much less understandable reasons.

"Tom, maybe what you say will help some other people avoid divorce, or give them strength," she suggested.

Bit by bit, he explained his feelings to her: "I really loved Carol a lot. I had dated quite a few girls before I got married, and decided that once I got married, it would be for keeps. We made a vow before God, and I wasn't going to leave my wife. True, I didn't expect such trouble right away, but you do what you have to. You just don't think about it sometimes, you just do what's right.

"When things looked hopeless, it was terribly hard. Some of the things I had to do were awful for me, like changing bedpans and stuff, but you just do them. There weren't many people around who could really take care of Carol like I could. She had to be lifted and carried so much, and supported emotionally. If I left, what would she do? I couldn't leave her.

"At first, I talked to my family and friends about it. I could tell it upset them, so I just decided to keep things inside. I figured that complaining really didn't do a lot of good. Everybody was helpless, the doctors were, I was, Carol was.

"I just decided to stick it out. When things got really bad, I would tell myself, 'just one more week and you can take off for Alaska.' I wouldn't have gone, but that was my way of coping. I knew when the week was up, I would be able to take another, and another.

"Carol told me many times to leave, saying she wasn't any good as a wife to me. I knew she was upset and discouraged. At the time we didn't know how things would turn out. I really loved her, and didn't want to leave.

"Even though I yelled at her sometimes when things got too frustrating, I knew I wouldn't leave. I found myself getting annoyed sometimes when she felt sorry for herself. I told her to stop having a pity party. Then she would cry. I didn't say that very often, though, because she couldn't help getting down sometimes. I think she did very well emotionally, considering what she went through.

"Every time we heard about a possible cure, Carol looked into it. She just wouldn't give up. She kept saying I deserved a wife who could take care of me.

"I kept busy, and I worked long hours. I spent time with my family, and sometimes I went out with the guys from work.

"I didn't leave, because I made a promise to stay with her, for better or worse. That's when you take care of each other, when things are hard."

I was very touched when I read what Tom said.

We celebrated our fifth wedding anniversary in June 1982, and Tom is still as steady and strong as he was during the bad years. He's like a rock.

I still go to the hospital for treatments. I still tire easily. But step by step, God is taking care of me every day. He is teaching me, guiding me, loving me. And I praise him for it. Dressing Jeff, cooking and cleaning my house, walking into church with my husband, brushing my teeth, and dialing a telephone are miracles I will never take for granted again.

Despite their early skepticism, my doctors now know that PE is working. I began with at least two treatments a week. As my body has healed, they have become further and further apart. I may still need them; now they are months apart. After a few hours on the machine, I'm good until I need another "tune-up." I still take some medication, but plan to discontinue that also as soon as I can. I haven't had a treatment in seven months.

Some may say I wasn't healed. Some may say I would eventually have gotten better without all the prayer. I suppose it's possible, but I doubt it. I wouldn't have had the will to live. I wouldn't have had hope. Most of all, I wouldn't have come to know Jesus as Lord and realized that life here is merely a prelude to eternity.

After I was better, I was able to obtain and read my medical records. I was quite surprised at many of the crises and the doctors' predictions. There is still some disagreement among my doctors as to just what to call my condition. Some doctors called my condition recurring GBS; others, who believe GBS is acute (only one attack), termed it chronic, relapsing, inflammatory polyradiculoneuropathy—a similar condition, but chronic or recurring. My condition had been even worse than I realized. The diagnosis isn't as important to me as the fact that I am healing. And the scriptural promises of healing and salvation that I came to know, believe, and claim during my sickness were the key to my recovery.

I am convinced that the following healing Scriptures helped me on my road to recovery, both physically and spiritually:

I will take sickness away from the midst of thee (Exod. 23:25).

Bless the Lord, O my soul, and forget not all his benefits: Who forgiveth all thine iniquities; who healeth all thy diseases (Ps. 103:2-3).

He sent his word, and healed them (Ps. 107:20).

But he was wounded for our transgressions, he was bruised for our iniquities: the chastisement of our peace was upon him; and with his stripes we are healed (Isa. 53:5).

But unto you that fear my name shall the Sun of righteousness arise with healing in his wings (Mal. 4:2).

Jesus went about all Galilee, teaching in their synagogues, and preaching the gospel of the kingdom, and healing all manner of sickness and all manner of disease among the people (Matt. 4:23).

When the even was come, they brought unto him many that were possessed with devils: and he cast out the spirits with his word, and healed all that were sick: That it might be fulfilled which was spoken by Esaias the prophet, saying, Himself took our infirmities, and bare our sicknesses (Matt. 8:16-17).

My son, attend to my words; incline thine ear unto my sayings. Let them not depart from thine eyes; Keep them in the midst of thine heart. For they are life unto those that find them, and health to all their flesh (Prov. 4:20-22).

The prayer of faith shall save the sick, and the Lord shall raise him up (James 5:15).

. . . who his own self bare our sins in his own body on the tree, that we, being dead to sins, should live unto righteousness: by whose stripes ye were healed (1 Peter 2:24).

I always tried to pray with another Christian or two when I had specific requests. Matthew 18:19 says, "If two of you shall agree on earth as touching any thing that they shall ask, it shall be done for them of my Father which is in heaven."

Believe that it is God's will for you to be healed. Third John 2 states, "Beloved, I wish above all things that thou mayest prosper and be in health, even as thy soul prospereth."

Jeremiah 1:12 says, "I will hasten my word to perform it."

All of this may sound as though I used a magic formula, but it's not that way at all. These are promises, there in the Bible, for all to read and believe. I read them, believed them, claimed them, and prayed a lot. I gradually became better, through good doctors, good friends, and much prayer from others.

I encourage you to read these scripture passages from the Bible itself, not just from this page. Look them up; they are part of God's holy Word. Jesus Christ is the same yesterday, today, and tomorrow, and so is the Word of God.

I have been asked what would happen if I ever had another serious relapse. First, I don't think that will happen. But I don't sit and worry about it. The Bible says not to worry about tomorrow, and I try not to.

If I should find myself back in a state of paralysis, I have to admit that I would not be happy about it. Yet God has brought me back from that condition before, and I would trust that he had something in mind for me. Romans 8:28 says, "We know that all things work together for good to them that love God, to them who are the called according to his purpose." I believe that.

I also believe God's will is that we be well. Why some people, good and faithful Christians, are not healed is something I don't understand. I'll have to ask God about it when I get to heaven. I know that it doesn't mean their faith isn't strong enough. It's a mystery to me, and we just have to trust the Lord. It took years before we saw even the beginning of my healing, so sometimes healings aren't instant and miraculous, but a slow, long-term process that may take years and years.

Without the spiritual healing I received, I wouldn't have had peace about dying when I was so close to death. My two biggest fears, death and childbirth, are gone. I never understood death. Now I don't fear it, because I'll be with the Lord.

Each day as I walk around my home, as I hug and kiss my child, as I laugh with my husband, I thank God for giving me this new chance at life. Tom and I are living as normal a life as possible, and we are raising Jeffrey to know and love the Lord. Of course, he'll have to make his own choice when he gets older, but we plan to do all we can to teach him about the grace and love of God.

Cherry and banana cream pie are Tom's favorites, and I often bake them for him. I clean my house alone, do the laundry, sew, bake, and cook. Tom and I attend an active, Bible-teaching church, and I attend a daytime Bible study group. My friend Mary Ellen sometimes drives me to visit shut-ins and elderly people. I share my experiences with them and it seems to help them trust God in the midst of their trials. I've learned not to tell anyone that they don't have problems compared to mine. Each person's problems are unique, and serious enough to cause pain. We have to bear each other's burdens.

———◆———

After my fingers began working again, I dug out the latch-hook rug kit Bob and Charlene had given me on my birthday four years earlier when I was paralyzed. Then I was able only to breathe, swallow, talk, and type with a mouthstick. I was determined to hook that rug and give it back to them as a tangible symbol of the fulfillment of their act of faith.

"I have something for you," I announced to Bob and Charlene after I finished the rug.

I presented them with the colorful wall hanging. "The Lord Is My Shepherd" was spelled out in large, rounded letters. Charlene blinked back tears. "Praise the Lord," she said. "I knew you could do it."

I watched our son giggling at his father, looked at my dear friends, and remembered how many people had shown us love and care.

Now that the rug is finished, I still have one more promise to keep. Ray, the therapist who so long ago gave me the "He Lives" cross, also gave me instructions to hand that cross back to him someday. Now he has moved several thousand miles away. But I *will* hand that cross back to him sometime, and say, "I know. Jesus does live . . . and he cares."

This journey through life can sometimes be frightening and difficult, but faith, hope, and love make it easier and less lonely. I thank the Lord for answered prayer, for the promises of the Scriptures, and for fellow Christians who continued to encourage me and pray for me even when things looked the darkest. I am walking home in victory and gratitude.

EPILOGUE

March 1983

When Carol first began the experimental treatments for her condition, she needed several plasma exchange sessions per week. To the surprise and joy of her doctors at the University of Michigan hospitals, Carol has not required a plasma exchange treatment for an entire year. She's doing fine now, living at home, caring for her family, and learning more about the grace of God every day. She is strong enough to care for three-year-old Jeff—a mischievous, happy little boy—cook, clean her own home, and speak two or three times a week. Tom and Carol will celebrate their sixth wedding anniversary in a few months. They get plenty of exercise keeping up with their energetic toddler.

Most of Carol's closest friends are some of the women who helped her and her family through their ordeal. Carol treasures these precious, lasting friendships.

Carol's family physician, Dr. Thompson, has followed her condition since he first treated her in 1977. He considers her recovery miraculous and is sure she would have died without plasma exchange. A few months ago, she visited the doctor who had first told her she would be permanently quadriplegic. He looked at her in amazement. "You know, you're defying the medical reports. This is a miracle." She smiled back at him and said, "I know."